I WILL SING OF MY REDEEMER

Inspiring Devotions from 52
Great Hymns of the Faith

Dennis C Stevenson Jr
www.Dennis-Stevenson.com

Cover Art courtesy of German Creation

CONTENTS

INTRODUCTION

I grew up singing hymns in church. As a boy, I learned every verse of hundreds of songs. I liked to pretend I could read the notes and sing all the different parts (those around me might not have appreciated it very much). Singing these hymns defined what it meant to go to church.

Years later I look back on those great hymns and I am amazed by what a treasure they have been in my life. With age and perspective, I have a fresh appreciation for how they taught me who God is and how I ought to love Him.

There is something about hearing a piano play the introduction to one of these songs that immediately transports me back to a simpler time. Music has this ability to capture our hearts and imagination in a powerful way that grounds us to place and time.

As I reviewed the hymns in this book, I was shocked how many I could still sing. Often, I could sing multiple verses. The words simply flowed one after the other.

I have stored up your word in my heart,
that I might not sin against you.
Psalm 119:11

While the great hymns of our faith are not the same as God's word, they point directly to God's word. When we think of songs like Amazing Grace or Jesus Loves Me or Christ the Lord is Risen Today, the scripture almost jumps off the page.

These hymns are full of truth. They proclaim God's greatness. They celebrate God's love displayed in Jesus' willing sacrifice at the cross. They point to the practical matters of living a holy life in this fallen world. Again and again they return to the simple faith upon which our Christian lives are built.

I owe a debt of gratitude to the men and women who penned those lyrics. Someday in heaven I would like to thank them personally. Their contribution to my spiritual growth has been profound.

I wrote this book to celebrate these great hymns of our faith. Even though they have been replaced by more modern songs, they still have a lot to offer.

I've returned to those comforting and familiar words and explored the faith they proclaim. Each song is full of biblical truth that we need in our lives today. We would be wise to remember the lessons they have taught us. The Spirit of God will certainly use them to teach us new lessons again.

There are many ways you could use this book. You might want to read through and enjoy the pleasant trips down memory lane as each new hymn comes up. You might want to refresh your heart with the familiar words and spend time meditating on the spiritual truth they contain. You might use this as a guide for fifty two days or 52 weeks to lead your heart and mind to consider God and what He has done for you.

It's up to you.

My prayer is that you'll be inspired and humbled. Not because my words are so great, but because these great songs point back to our amazing God. You'll find scripture in every hymn. Use it to focus your attention on God and the tremendous effort He has displayed to show you how much He loves you.

I've developed a resource kit to help you enjoy this book and enhance its purpose of leading you back to God. I've assembled links to performances of all the hymns I shared in the book. I've also found the complete lyrics and linked to them as well. Finally, I developed a devotional workbook should you want to journal or reflect more deeply on the truth these songs teach us about God.

You can get this resource kit for free on my website at **https://dennis-stevenson.com/HymnResources**. I hope you take advantage of it. I really enjoyed researching and picking each of the songs to share with you.

Most of all, I hope you enjoy these great hymns and let them remind you of the Redeemer who has ransomed your life.

Bless the LORD, O my soul,
and all that is within me,
bless his holy name!
Psalm 103:1

I WILL SING OF MY REDEEMER

I will sing of my Redeemer,
And His wondrous love to me.
On the cruel cross He suffered,
From the curse to set me free.
Sing oh sing, of my Redeemer,
With His blood, He purchased me.
 On the cross, He sealed my pardon,
Paid the debt, and made me free.

Philip P. Bliss

S ing a song to your Redeemer. Lift up His name and be glad. Rejoice for He has purchased you back from slavery and death and given you a glorious new future.

Therefore the redeemed of the LORD shall return, and come with singing unto Zion; and everlasting joy shall be upon their head: they shall obtain gladness and joy; and sorrow and mourning shall flee away.
Isaiah 51:11

This great hymn draws our attention to our Redeemer. Jesus, the Son of God, gave Himself for us so that we could find peace with God. He exchanged His glory and majesty for a human life and suffered and died a humiliating death as a criminal when He had done nothing wrong.

We were lost, dead in our sins, and unable to do anything to earn God's favor. But Jesus came to earth and traded places with us, giving us His righteousness and taking the penalty for our sins.

No matter how hard we try, we cannot escape the centrality of the gospel in our lives. Because God loved us, we have a future instead of everlasting punishment. Because Jesus said "Not as I will, but as You will," (Matthew 26:39) and accepted the shame of the cross, we stand before God clothed in His righteousness.

> The saying is trustworthy and deserving of full
> acceptance, that Christ Jesus came into the world to
> save sinners, of whom I am the foremost.
> 1 Timothy 1:15

As sinners we lived under a guilty verdict. From the very first moment of our lives, we were contaminated by sin and offensive to God. We could do nothing on our own to change our status before God. Our first sin sealed our fate.

Yet while we were in this terrible situation, Jesus came. He did not ask us to clean ourselves up. He did not demand a certain level acceptable behavior before He would entertain our salvation. While we were indelibly stained by our sin and rebellion, He took our place and gave us His righteousness.

Now we stand before God as sons and daughters. We have an inheritance with His Son. We have a home prepared for us in Heaven and the Holy Spirit of God dwells in us as the guarantee that everything we have not yet received will come to pass.

We have received such a wonderful gift. It must change us and change our perspective. This song calls upon us to express love to our Redeemer in song. Let us respond to Him with the love that He showed to us in the first place.

> We love Him because He first loved us.
> 1 John 4:19

We cannot match the grandness of His display of love. We do not need to. We aren't trying to pay Him back. It was a gift of grace. (Ephesians 2:8-9) Our response is to receive it and give all glory back to Him.

Singing seems like so little in contrast to the great gift we have received. As the song reminds us of the suffering and pain He endured on our behalf, it seems like we should do much more. Yet this is the great wonder of the gospel. We could not work our way to redemption on our own. Nor can we pay back the price of the gift we have received.

Instead, let us turn our attention to the glory of God and His Son, Jesus Christ. Let us point our lives toward Him and declare His majesty. He is great and greatly to be praised. It is right that we stop and sing of our Redeemer. Let us talk daily of His wondrous love.

I will praise my dear Redeemer;
His triumphant power I'll tell,
How the victory He giveth
Over sin and death and hell.

A MIGHTY FORTRESS IS OUR GOD

A mighty fortress is our God
A bulwark never failing;
Our helper He amid the flood
Of mortal ills prevailing.
For still our ancient foe
Doth seek to work us woe
His craft and power are great,
And, armed with cruel hate,
On earth is not His equal.

Martin Luther

What image comes to mind when you sing of a "mighty fortress" or a "bulwark"? Do you think of the great castles that were built in Europe? Surely Martin Luther had these in mind when he penned these lyrics. Living in Germany, he would have seen mighty stone fortifications.

This is the picture that we are invited to associate with our God. A mighty castle soaring high into the air with thick walls built of stone. It was the place to which everyone could run when an attack came. When the countryside became dangerous and troubled, it was a safe place to go.

This song is unique because of the attention it gives to our ancient foe. By this, we most certainly think of our old enemy, Satan. He is powerful. We cannot deny that. The song simply states it. His motivation is hatred toward anything associated with God.

In the face of such a foe, we are certainly not safe on our own. As we go about our lives, we have no natural resistance for such an implacable enemy. We live in the land of danger.

The attacks of our opponent are many. Whether it be the temptation to sin, or bodily sickness, or ridicule at work, or even strained relationships across our family, Satan is capable of great affliction. Like a roaring lion, he stalks about seeking whom he may devour (1 Peter 5:8).

Fortunately, we are not set loose on our own, encouraged to fare well, and expected to overcome the devil on our own. Even the Apostle Paul, writing specifically about the spiritual warfare that rages around us, encourages us to "stand firm." (Ephesians 6:18)

Jesus Himself brings us back to the grounding truth when He says "Take heart, I have overcome the world." (John 16:33)

It is to the mighty fortress of Jesus' power that we run. Under His wings, we find safety and security. No matter how the world rages about us, how Satan stalks our lives, and our hearts, Jesus' power is overcoming power.

Long before Martin Luther, the Psalmist wrote in Psalm 46:

> God is our refuge and strength,
>   a very present help in trouble.
> Therefore we will not fear though the earth gives way,
>   though the mountains be moved into the heart of the
> sea,
> though its waters roar and foam,

though the mountains tremble at its swelling.
Selah

What trouble surrounds you today? What seems greater than anything you can handle under your power? You don't have to bear it alone. Run to the mighty fortress that is our God. Find security and safety under his protection.

We are not alone, and this great hymn reminds us of that great truth. We have a safe place to which we can retreat when the attack comes and the opposition grows too great. We can rely upon the power of our God to defend us from all attackers.

Sing this song to yourself today. Take encouragement from the triumphant tune. It exudes confidence in our fortress and bulwark. It confirms that our defense is a sure thing because our God is so great.

Verse 3 returns to this theme and makes a bold promise:

And though this world with devils filled
Should threaten to undo us,
We will not fear, for God has willed
His truth to triumph through us.
The prince of darkness grim,
We tremble not for him -
His rage we can endure,
For lo his doom is sure:
One little word shall fell him.

One little word will bring total victory. One statement from the lips of our mighty King will bring the conflict to an end. On earth is not His equal!

Praise God from Whom All Blessings Flow

Praise God from whom all blessings flow,
Praise Him all creatures here below.
Praise Him above, ye heavenly host.
Praise Father, Son and Holy Ghost.
Amen.

Thomas Ken

Many people know this song as the Doxology. It began as the refrain to two separate hymns written by Thomas Ken. However, these four melodic lines have continued to achieve far greater fame than the original verses that accompanied them.

By either name, this song is loaded with the spiritual truth that we would do well to remember.

Prominent throughout the song is the command to praise God. Each line begins with this command, lest we forget our duty to praise. Praise is our appropriate response to God.

He is exalted above us. His thoughts are not our thoughts. His plan for the world is so broad and comprehensive that we cannot fathom it. His love displayed toward us is so unexpected and gracious that we can never grow tired of it.

So we must praise. Praise with our voice, as in singing this song. Praise with our lips as we speak throughout the day. Praise with our attitude throughout the day, remembering what God has done for us.

As we sing this song, we align ourselves with the Psalmist who wrote in Psalm 150:

> Praise the LORD!
> Praise God in his sanctuary;
>   praise Him in his mighty heavens!
> Praise Him for his mighty deeds;
>   praise Him according to his excellent greatness!
> Praise Him with trumpet sound;
>   praise Him with lute and harp!
> Praise Him with tambourine and dance;
>   praise Him with strings and pipe!
> Praise Him with sounding cymbals;
>   praise Him with loud clashing cymbals!
> Let everything that has breath praise the LORD!
> Praise the LORD!

Whether you look forward to your day or back upon it, this song reminds us to do so with an attitude that is full of praise.

Yet this is not all that we stand to gain from this simple melody.

The first line boldly states that all blessings flow from God. How often do we think that the blessings we receive come as a result of our hard work, or our hard-won skill? No. This verse reminds of James 1:17 where James writes that all good gifts come from above.

When we believe that all gifts come from God, we are positioned in a dependent posture. We need God. He is the source of goodness in our lives - not ourselves, our work, or our family, or whatever else you might be tempted to substitute. Rightly identifying God as the gift giver focuses our attention on Him as we go through our day. Anticipation for His goodness in our lives is a strong motivation to keep Him in the center of our attention.

Recognizing God as the source of goodness in our life gives us further motivation to praise Him. It also helps us resist the temptation to praise ourselves. We were not responsible for whatever good thing happened to us. God is.

Every creature owes God for their existence. That alone should be cause for praise. But even beyond that, the Angels praise God because they see Him in all his glory and majesty. They know who He is. They also see how He deals with humanity, and are amazed as it puts His goodness on display. We, here on earth, ought also to praise God. We are the recipient of His mercy and grace. Our eternal futures are secured by His sacrifice, we are granted righteousness that we did not earn. We receive forgiveness whenever we ask. There are so many reasons for us to lift God in praise.

Finally, the song reminds us of the triune God. We are commanded to praise God (the Father), Son, and Holy Ghost. God is Three in One, living in a harmonious community across eternity. Praise God whose plan is good and laid the plan for our redemption. Praise the Son who voluntarily went to the cross and paid our price. Praise the Spirit who lives within us and serves as the down payment of the benefits we have yet to receive.

Let this familiar tune stick in your head and remind you throughout your day to praise God.

FAIREST LORD JESUS

Fairest Lord Jesus, Ruler of all nature,
O Thou of God and man the Son.
Thee will I cherish; Thee will I honor,
Thou my soul's glory, joy, and crown

Anonymous

J ust the first verse alone of this song is packed with deep
spiritual truth about Jesus Christ. If we could elevate our
thinking to simply review these lyrics throughout the day,
we would be doing a wonderful act of meditation and
devotion.

The first word itself is a challenge to our ordinary way of
thinking: Fairest. Our everyday pattern is not that we think
poorly of our Lord Jesus, but that we do not think of Him at
all. To be reminded, and to remind ourselves, of how
wonderful He is would be a rewarding line of thought any
day of the week. Not only does this great hymn begin with
the sweet notion of the beauty of Jesus, but it also goes on to
unpack that loveliness in tender detail.

The first description of Jesus focuses on His sovereignty and
lordship. He is the ruler of all nature. Indeed He rules it

because He created it. The Apostle Paul picks up this same sentiment in his letter to the Colossians.

> For by Him all things were created, in heaven and on earth, visible and invisible, whether thrones or dominions or rulers or authorities-all things were created through Him and for Him. And He is before all things, and in Him all things hold together. Colossians 1:16-17

This is no small Jesus. This is Jesus wrapped in his power as God almighty.

The next line delves into the mystery of the incarnation. Jesus is fully God and human at the same time. This mystery boggles even the wisest minds, except that we know it to be true. And we should be grateful for it. For only someone fully human could be offered as our substitution sacrifice. And only someone fully divine could live the perfect life of obedience needed to fulfill the law.

The last half of the verse leads us into our worshipful response to these truths.

Thee will I cherish. The word itself might be a little old fashioned. It's not one we use regularly today. But we know it means to love. Perhaps another word for it might be to treasure. It means that we believe there is great value in something, and as a consequence, we hold it very dear because of that value. Indeed, Jesus is valuable. What could be more? Do you hold Him dear?

Thee will I honor. This is a timeless sentiment. But to honor someone means to hold them in high esteem, to look up to them. Is that how you see Jesus? Are you continually looking up to Him? It is an appropriate position. If you struggle for this vantage point, try falling to your knees.

This verse wraps up with a personal summary of what Jesus meant to the songwriter. It's an invitation for us to respond in the same way.

Jesus is the one thing that lifts our soul and makes it glorious, for, without Him, our soul is lost and under divine judgment. Jesus is the only one who can bring joy to our souls. And at the end of all time, Jesus is our great reward. In the New Jerusalem, we will no longer worship Him from afar and in spirit, but we shall see Him face to face.

Meditate on Jesus today. Hum the tune of this song to remind yourself that indeed, He is the fairest of them all.

ALAS! AND DID MY SAVIOR BLEED

Alas! and did my Savior bleed
And did my Sovereign die?
Would He devote that sacred head,
For such a worm as I.

Isaac Watts

L ike many of the great hymns of old, this song brings us immediately to the foot of the cross. Oh, that we would visit this wonderful yet terrible site with greater frequency! When we gaze upon the sacrifice of our Lord, all of life's priorities fall into order.

In two brief sentences, Isaac Watts captures the glory and the terror of the cross. In the first, we see the sacrifice. Our Savior and Sovereign, broken and bleeding ultimately giving Himself as a sacrifice that He did not deserve. In the second, we see the beneficiary of this sacrifice. From the base of the cross, we see ourselves, unworthy of such a kingly offering.

This is the essence of the gospel. The glorious God, living eternally in light and perfection stepped down from His throne and entered the toil and suffering of this world. Amid the dirt and the darkness of the daily grind He lived in perfection, not to bring glory to Himself, but to sacrifice Himself for us and give the benefits of His life away to those who had already, repeatedly, defiantly disqualified themselves from such rewards.

Ultimately our Lord was glorified. His name cannot remain low. Despite sitting at the right hand of the Father today, He offers the benefits of His sacrifice to us today.

We do not deserve it. Repeatedly we have rejected it. Compared to His glory and perfection we are less than worms. Yet despite the apparent injustice, notwithstanding the radical inequity of the trade, He takes on our sin and gives us His perfection.

We give up the destiny we could not avoid and gain the inheritance we do not deserve.

Considering the gospel brings us low. Not back into the rebellion of our sinfulness, but bowed deeply in humility. When we consider what the cross did for us, we are oriented on the mercy and love of God. Our lives can no longer be about us, because we are the reason such a sacrifice had to happen.

For those who have received such generosity, how can we respond appropriately? It is not enough that we should assume the role of the debtor and begin the toil of "working off the debt of love" that we have received. By this sacrifice and gift, we have been elevated to the privileged position of sons and daughters. It is not for a son or daughter to attempt to repay the generosity of our Father.

The Apostle Paul puts it very well in his letter to the Corinthians:

> "You are not your own, for you were bought with a
> price. So glorify God in your body."
> 1 Corinthians 6:20

Glorify God. That is our response.

The Apostle John, beloved friend of Jesus, replies,

> "We love Him because He first loved us."
> 1 John 4:19

We love in return.

Isaac Watts did not leave us bowed at the cross, crushed by such a great sacrifice we could never repay. The fifth stanza brings us full circle.

But drops of grief can ne'er repay
The debt of love I owe;
Here, Lord, I give myself away,
'Tis all that I can do.

Our response to the sacrifice is to give ourselves away. We offer up our lives, not in repayment but as a gift of thanks. These lives are not our own. They have been purchased and are the possession of our Lord Jesus. So we give them back to Him, for His purpose and His glory.

'Tis all that we can do.

I SING THE MIGHTY POWER OF GOD

I sing the mighty power of God
That made the mountains rise;
That spread the flowing seas abroad
And built the lofty skies.
I sing the wisdom that ordained
The sun to rule the day;
The moon shines full at His command
And all the stars obey.

Isaac Watts

I n three verses, Isaac Watts takes a musical stroll through all of creation and reminds us that it all came into being through the action of God. The first stanza addresses the big elements that He created: mountains, seas, sun, moon, and stars.

In the second verse, the song turns toward food and the creatures that inhabit the planet. Very wisely the songwriter observes;

Lord, how Thy wonders are displayed
Wher'er I turn my eye;

If I survey the ground I tread
Or gaze upon the sky.

God's creative wonder is all around us. Wherever we look, we see it, whether it's in the beauty of a sunset or the crisp freshness of a morning. If we have a place we like to visit in the mountains or by a lake, stream or the ocean. Just lifting our head to see the sun or the moon points us toward God.

The song first celebrates the power of God. It takes a power beyond anything we humans can know or understand to create the world out of nothing. If you imagine the most powerful thing that we have ever done, it pales in comparison to the amazing power of God's creation. We still haven't fully defined the full expanse of the universe He created, but He spoke it all into existence with a word.

Yet despite the amazing extent of God's creation, He also had the attention to detail to create beautiful flowers, sunsets, and waterfalls. God did not create a mass production factory of creation that turned out boring products. He is a master craftsman and all of His creation bears the results of His skill.

The song also speaks of God's wisdom in creation. Not only did He call it into existence, but He did so in a way that works for us to live. We exist on a planet that rotates, with sun and moon to light the day and night and cause tides that circulate the waters of the seas.

God had a wise purpose and plan that guided His creation. He designed this world so that we could live on it. He made it suitable to support our lives. As we study our environment, we are beginning to understand all the myriad of ways that this Earth supports us. We learn how we are perfectly suited to the planet and it to us.

In the second verse, we sing of the goodness of the Lord. This celebrates His provision for us. He has created a world that has food and animals for our use. He did not create us and expect us to create our nourishment but provided it to us. And what sustenance! Not only does it supply the nutrition that our bodies need, but it also tastes delicious.

In His goodness, God created a world that is pleasant and enjoyable. There are many things that we partake of that draw us back again and again for the sheer enjoyment of it. Not only did He create a pleasing world, but He created us to be able to take pleasure in it.

The prophet Jeremiah summarizes this idea well.

> "It is He who made the earth by his power,
>   who established the world by his wisdom,
>   and by his understanding stretched out the heavens.
> When He utters his voice there is a tumult of waters in the heavens,
> And He makes the mist rise from the ends of the earth.
> He makes lightning for the rain,
>   and He brings forth the wind from his storehouses."
> Jeremiah 51:15

So we sing. We remember God and His power and His wisdom and His goodness. We give all glory back to Him.

As you go about your day, notice the power and wisdom and goodness of God about you. He is there, waiting to be seen.

O GOD, OUR HELP IN AGES PAST

O God, our Help in ages past,
Our Hope for years to come,
Our Shelter from the stormy blast
And our eternal Home!

Isaac Watts

Oh, how often we forget the truth of this great hymn when life closes in around us. Difficult times come upon us and we flounder, seeking a strong anchor to center us, yet find only shifting sand. Self-reliance, often praised, offers us neither solidity nor peace when our circumstances become challenging.

The best answer is to turn back to God. Only in Him do we find the protection we need to weather the storms that confront us daily. This song gently guides us back to our only refuge and reminds us of the truths that console us in our times of trouble.

Remember that God has been our help before. Help is His nature for those who love Him. In His tender care for us, He is consistent, helping us when we need aid. Do you keep a journal? Perhaps it would make sense to start recording the times that God has helped you. This way when hard times come again, you can review God's steady track record of care over you.

In extreme times, turn to your Bible. The writer to the Hebrews cries out "See how we are surrounded by so great a cloud of witnesses!" Is your life more desperate than the children of Israel in Egypt? Is your loss greater than the widow of Zarephath whose only son died? Is your health worse than the woman who suffered bleeding for twelve years?

Look into your Bible and see these stories played out where God came to the help of these faithful saints. He has intervened in tremendous trouble and brought from those circumstances light and joy. Your situation is not beyond His power. Take hope!

Remember that God is our hope for the future. When tomorrow seems dark and forbidding, God brings light and love to our eyes. Whether it's the anticipation of His help in the troubles that lie ahead, or if it's the greater blessing that comes when we are finally reunited with Him in glory. God does not leave us alone on this Earth to find our way. He promises to be with us always and to see the journey complete, to its final destination - with Him forever.

Do not become obsessed with the things that might happen in the future. Fall back on God to see you through them. This does not mean He will make the hard times go away, but He will remain with you through them. He promises to use even your worst circumstance to bring about good and His glory. Rely upon these words of Jesus, "Fear not, for I have overcome the world." (John 16:33)

God is our shelter when the world seems to be a storm about us. As a shelter, He brings hope and help to our situation. We cannot be touched when we take cover in His arms, except that He permits it. And even then His power sustains us to receive the strength we need to endure.

The world may throw its worst at us, but our Shelter will hold firm. He cannot be moved or swayed by the tempest of trouble around us. His strength is directed toward us and our safety when we most need it.

God is our eternal home. Over this life lies the promise of Jesus "I go to prepare a place for you." (John 14:6) Our home awaits. We need not fear that we should find ourselves at the end of life in some strange or unwelcoming place. We shall be in the very place prepared for us by Jesus.

No matter what strange turns occur in your life, you will find yourself at the proper place when all is over. And when you arrive, such will be the joy of the presence of God that all the suffering in this life will seem of little consequence compared to the glory that you will experience.

Do not give up hope because that future seems so far away. Many of the benefits of that await us have already been made available. The Holy Spirit already lives within us, comforting and interceding. Our sins have been paid for, and God extends an offer of fellowship. It will be even better when we are in His presence. That's what we have to look forward to. But the help, hope and shelter we experience today give us confidence that better things are waiting for us in His presence.

AND CAN IT BE THAT I SHOULD GAIN?

And Can it be that I should gain,
An interest in the Savior's blood?
Died He for me, who caused His pain?
For me, who Him to death pursued?
Amazing love! How can it be
That Thou, my God, shoudst die for me?

Charles Wesley

C ould the gospel be stated any more plainly? Charles Wesley puts it poetically and simply. Jesus' sacrifice paid the penalty for my sin. He went to the cross instead of me. In exchange, He gave me His holiness and His righteousness. Now I am invited to stand before Almighty God and call Him "Daddy."

The song seems to burst out with the response: Amazing love!

Indeed, the love of God is amazing. It is beyond all human understanding or comprehension. Love that gives when it seems that punishment is appropriate. Love that embraces when it should push away. Love that pays when it should collect.

How often do you cry out in your spirit "Amazing love!"?

Is it real to you? Does it rest upon your shoulders daily? Do you remember it as you go about the ordinary tasks of your day?

The love of God should ever be in our vision. We have been the recipients of the most wonderful gift imaginable. It carries the true price tag of "priceless". There is no way in heaven or earth that we could acquire such love on our own.

No act of generosity could overcome our debt. No act of sacrifice could offset our sin. No act of penance could gain us favor in God's sight.

Yet it pleased Him to send His Son to live among us and to spill that divine blood upon a rugged cross of shame. And we are the beneficiaries. We gain a substantial interest in the grace that flowed out of Jesus' sacrifice. We receive grace that is greater than all of our sins.

Often we must face up to the dreadful bad news before we can fully appreciate the delightful good news. This song leads us gently through the bad and rejoices in the wonderful. We who were lost have been found. We who were poor have become immeasurably wealthy in Christ. We who were enemies have become family.

What better way to begin your day than with a reminder of the amazing love of God? Or perhaps you should end your day meditating upon this blessed gift? Maybe you should rejoice in the reality of your salvation in the middle of your day.

The truth is that God did die for us, even though we did not deserve it. As the Apostle Paul says in his letter to the Romans:

> For while we were still weak, at the right time Christ died for the ungodly. For one will scarcely die for a righteous person-though perhaps for a good person one would dare even to die- but God shows his love for us in that while we were still sinners, Christ died for us. Romans 5:6-8

Let this song be your anthem. Ask the questions - but with confidence in the answers. Yes, God's love is amazing. And it is ours. And there's nothing that we need to do but accept it and trust in Jesus to do the rest.

O FOR A THOUSAND TONGUES TO SING

O for a thousand tongues to sing
My great Redeemer's praise,
The glories of my God and king,
The triumphs of His grace!

Charles Wesley

I t is a biological fact that we only have one tongue and one voice for speaking and singing. In this song, Mr. Wesley wishes it were not so and imagines that we had a thousand tongues and could speak with a thousand voices. Then, he declares, that he would direct every voice to the harmonious celebration of one thing: praising God.

That is an attitude that we should try to emulate. Such a passionate pursuit of praise speaks volumes toward that which we would praise. Do you agree with this sentiment? Would you offer such praise to your Redeemer?

Too often, we are distracted by the cares of this world. The apparent urgency of matters in our daily life crowds out those things of supreme importance. Praising God falls victim to these misshapen priorities.

This stanza offers a three-fold reason to lift our voices daily in praise.

God has redeemed us. We, who were lost in our trespasses and sins, have been purchased back to Him at the most expensive price imaginable. God did not turn aside from bringing His full wrath upon Jesus. He poured upon His Son the full measure of the just anger that we deserve. Yet towards us He turns His eyes of love. If anything is praise-worthy, this must be at the top of the list.

This, of course, leads us to sing of God's glory. Having been redeemed, we gaze upon the perfection of His holiness. We acknowledge Him as our king, our sovereign, our ruler. We joyfully follow His new law, which He has written in our hearts (Jeremiah 31:33). Therefore, we exalt in His banner over us. What tongue would hesitate to sing His praises?

God's grace is continually poured out toward us. When we sin, He forgives us and restores the relationship that has been damaged. (1 John 1:9) He brings about all things for good in our lives. He hears our prayers and delights to answer us. He grants us victorious power over sin and gives us a new desire to live for Him.

The fourth stanza doubles down on the delight of praising God.

Hear Him, ye deaf, His praise, ye dumb,
Your loosened tongues employ;
Ye blind, behold your Savior come,
And leap ye lame for joy.

The praise of God overwhelms any limitation that we might think holds us back. Such is its urgency and its power. We cannot do anything but praise. We will not stop for any lesser goal than proclaiming the greatness of our God.

How are you today? Do you feel the goodness of God in your life?

Even if this day is one of trouble and persecution, remember what God has done for you. The price of your sin has been paid. Your estrangement from God has been replaced with family bonds. Your future has been upgraded to an inheritance with Christ. You have been given the Holy Spirit as a down payment toward all the things that you have not yet received in full.

We have but one tongue. Today let it be dedicated toward the praise of our one God and our King.

Join with David when he says in:

> Let those who delight in my righteousness
> shout for joy and be glad
> and say evermore,
> "Great is the LORD,
> who delights in the welfare of his servant!"
> Then my tongue shall tell of your righteousness
> and of your praise all the day long.
> Psalm 35:27-28

CHRIST THE LORD IS RISEN TODAY

Christ the Lord is risen today, Alleluia!
Sons of men and angels say: Alleluia!
Raise your joys and triumphs high, Alleluia!
Sing, ye heavens and earth, reply: Alleluia!

Charles Wesley

A familiar song to be sung at Easter, this anthem celebrates a truth that is welcome any day of the year. The title of the song proclaims the great truth around which all of our faith hangs. The Apostle Paul put it most pointedly in his letter to the Corinthians:

> And if Christ has not been raised, then our preaching is
> in vain and your faith is in vain.
> 1 Corinthians 15:14

Mary, Peter, and John saw the empty tomb. Jesus appeared in the locked upper room to the eleven disciples. Paul reports that up to five hundred people saw Him at one time. He has risen!

The premise seems illogical. Death, the implacable foe of all humanity, has been defeated. The grave has been forced to give up its possession. But that is what we celebrate as Christians.

> "O death, where is your victory?
> O death, where is your sting?"
> 1 Corinthians 15:55

Christ has defeated the power of death.

The statement seems ridiculous. When our friends and loved ones die, they do not come back to us. They are gone forever, and we grieve their loss. But with Jesus, it is not so. He died at Calvary. He was buried in a grave, sealed by the might of the Roman Empire. But He did not remain. Three days later He rose triumphantly.

Jesus' resurrection is of world-shaking importance. For the believer, it is the great game-changer. If Jesus can defeat death, then He has the power and the authority to offer the same to us. Death does not hold dominion over us.

When dealing with the scepticism of the Pharisees regarding His power, Jesus said,

> "Why do you question in your hearts? Which is easier, to say, 'Your sins are forgiven you,' or to say, 'Rise and walk'? But that you may know that the Son of Man has authority on earth to forgive sins," He said to the man who was paralysed. "I say to you, rise, pick up your bed and go home." And immediately he rose up before them and picked up what he had been lying on and went home, glorifying God.
> Luke 5:22-24

So when Jesus said "I give unto them eternal life," how can we know that He can do this? We need only look to the empty grave. In the empty grave, the power of God is on display for all to see.

The song seems to break out into spontaneous exultation in the four-fold "Alleluia!" Indeed, what other response is appropriate? For upon hearing the news that even though we shall die, yet shall we live forever in glory with God, what other outbursts could we utter?

"Amen!" "Praise God!" "Alleluia!"

If Jesus can conquer death, what can He do with the circumstances of your life? He has visibly demonstrated the greater miracle. How trivial it must be for Him to perform lesser miracles for us.

Rejoice today that Christ has risen from the dead. In doing so, He offers you the promise of life eternal with Him. He demonstrates the full measure of God's power over sin and death, which translates to power over the smaller challenges in our lives.

And if you find yourself singing "Alleluia" for no apparent reason today, sing it with gusto!

WHEN MORNING GILDS THE SKIES

When morning gilds the skies,
My heart awaking cries
"May Jesus Christ be praised!"
Alike at work and prayer,
To Jesus I repair;
"May Jesus Christ be praised!"

Katholisches Gesangbuch

D awn is a wonderful time. When we see the sun coloring the eastern horizon, we might think of God painting a beautiful picture across the sky. The morning is a time for wonder and for new beginnings.

What do you think about when you first wake up? How about during the middle of a busy day?

This great hymn draws us back to what it means to live a life centered in worship. That is what the cry "May Jesus Christ be praised!" is about.

We all want to cultivate a worshipful attitude that endures throughout our day. We sing these words and they pull against our hearts, reminding us of this goal. Morning, noon, and night we are singing praises to our Savior.

Indeed, Jesus is worthy of such praise. Of this, there can be no doubt or wavering of any sort.

Only Jesus set aside the glories of heaven and the power of His divinity to life a life as a servant. Paul writes eloquently of this in Philippians chapter 2. As humans, we cannot fully grasp the magnitude of what He set aside when He came to Earth.

Only Jesus lived a life that fully satisfied God's holy law. Without sin, He endured every temptation that we have encountered, and He weathered it to the very end, without giving in. We could never do it ourselves. Before we were even aware of the need, we had already blown our opportunity many times over. Jesus, however, resisted every opportunity to fall short of God's glory. (Hebrews 4:15)

Only Jesus died a terrible sinner's death when He deserved the exact opposite. On the cross He cried out in ultimate agony "My God! My God! Why have you forsaken me?" (Matthew 27:46) He endured a severing of the divine unity because He was taking the consequence for things He had not done and sins that He did not commit.

Only Jesus sits on the right hand of God, daily interceding for us as our advocate. (1 John 2:1) When the evil one tries to point to our sins, Jesus points to His hands and says "I paid for that." How many times must He say that every day?

Only Jesus shares His inheritance with us. In Romans 8, the Apostle Paul calls us "heirs of God and joint-heirs with Jesus." The Apostle Peter speaks of our "inheritance that is imperishable, undefiled, and unfading." We did not come by this through our fleshly birth. Only through our re-birth could we gain such a benefit.

We could go on for pages with "Only Jesus" statements. He is worthy of all the praise that we can offer and more. We will never exhaust the extent of His worthiness.

In the middle of His Triumphal Entry into Jerusalem the final time, Jesus acknowledged the importance of praise. When the religious leaders got offended that His disciples and the crowd were singing praises about Him, He answered "I tell you that if these [the worshiping crowd] were silent, the very stones would cry out." (Luke 19:40)

So the song encourages us to remember this throughout our day. We are instructed to give voice to our praise in exclamations of honor and glory to Him.

Praise must happen. He is worthy. If not us, then the rocks on the ground will give voice to His praise. How much better, and appropriate, that we sing His praise?

COME, THOU FOUNT OF EVERY BLESSING

Come, Thou fount of every blessing,
Tune my heart to sing thy grace.
Streams of mercy never ceasing,
Call for songs of loudest praise.
Teach me some melodious sonnet,
Sung by flaming tongues above.
Praise the mount! I'm fixed upon it,
Mount of God's unchanging love.

Robert Robinson

What a beautiful picture! You and I rooted to a rugged mountain, songs of praise pouring from our mouths like streams of water, inspired by the Holy Spirit who dances like a flame above our heads at Pentecost. All this is a grand entreaty for God to come and teach us how to sing more beautifully of His grace.

This fantastic old hymn opens with a simple request that God would come and change our hearts. God is the source of everything good in our lives (James 1:17). Therefore any change that He brings would be good for us. We do not place any constraints upon this change and accept them gladly.

The hymn uses the picture of tuning our hearts as we would tune an instrument. The notion of "tuning my heart" recognizes that our hearts are out of tune and need divine attention. We are not where we want to be. Thank God we're not where we were! But we cannot sit back and rest. We need the Fount of blessings to come and use His divine tuning fork to remove discord and harmonize our hearts.

What is the subject of this great song? God's grace. In one word the songwriter wraps up the entirety of the gospel, our new position as co-heirs with Jesus, and our eternal future with God. Grace: God's Riches At Christ's Expense. It is a beautiful package that we cannot earn, but can only receive.

When we think about God's grace, we should break out in song. We should sing endlessly of the greatness of God who provided it for us. That's how wonderful grace is.

Instead of enemies, we are sons and daughters. Instead of condemned, we are accepted. Instead of filthy, we are clean and clothed in white.

We will not receive what we deserve - which is the very picture of mercy. It flows all around us like a stream. In every aspect of our life, mercy is applied and we find ourselves passing what we actually deserve over to Jesus, who paid the full price.

All of this mercy and grace are firmly rooted and will not move. The songwriter describes it as a mountain. If there is one thing we understand about a mountain, it won't move. It doesn't pick up and go far away. No, we think of mountains as having roots that penetrate deeply into the earth.

This is just like God's love. It is not fickle and moveable. It does not come and go. It is just as stable and fixed as a mountain. And this love is the source of all the blessings we receive. God's grace and mercy flow out of His love for us (Romans 5:8).

Praise God that His attitude toward us is based upon His love! It does not depend upon anything that we have done. For if it did, it would not be like a mountain. It would be like the storm-tossed ocean, always moving and in motion. No, God's love flows out of God's unchangeable character toward us. And that in itself is a good gift.

As you go about your day today, think back upon this simple request. Come, God, and change my heart to be ever aware of your grace. Make me sing an inspired song that tells of Your unfathomable mercy toward me.   Ground me in Your unchanging love.

Make that your prayer. Meditate upon this thought: God's love, mercy, and grace flowing through your life.

Oh, to grace how great a debtor,
Daily I'm constrained to be!
Let thy grace, Lord, like a fetter,
Bind my wand'ring heart to Thee:
Prone to wander, Lord I feel it,
Prone to leave the God I love.
Here's my heart, Lord, take and seal it,
Seal it for Thy courts above.

THERE IS A FOUNTAIN

There is a fountain filled with blood
Drawn from Immanuel's veins;
And sinners plunged beneath that flood,
Lose all their guilty stains:
Lose all their guilty stains,
Lose all their guilty stains;
And sinners plunged beneath that flood,
Lose all their guilty stains.

William Cowper

How strange it seems to sing a song whose lyric celebrates a fountain of blood. To say this is odd in our culture seems quite the understatement. Yet upon reflection, this is a lovely song with a message that cannot be understated.

These lyrics center upon one word that too often we ignore: guilty. As sinners, we stand before our God condemned and guilty. It is not a question and there is not another option available to us in our strength.

Many think wishfully that perhaps it's not a judgment but a balance, and some amount of good behavior can offset our guilty actions. Yet that is not the case, for James says

"Whoever keeps the whole law but fails in one point has become guilty of all of it." (James 2:10). Partial obedience is not obedience at all.

This song cuts straight to the heart of the matter and labels us guilty, stained with the actions that have offended God.

Yet it is in the context of our guilty stains that the prospect of a fountain of blood loses its horror. Perhaps it is our natural diminishment of sin that causes us to forget that to God, sin is a deadly offense. God has decreed that only in shed blood can the problem of sin ever be addressed. (Hebrews 9:22).

In the Old Testament we read of the sacrificial system which God established to address the sins of the nation of Israel. But in our minds, we edit that image to some abstract concept of sacrifice. We skip over the messy reality that animals died and their blood stayed the judgment of God.

The fundamental issue of the sacrificial system was that it was temporary. It could not fully or finally deal with the issue of sin. It pointed forward to the Final Sacrifice. Those who offered animal sacrifice placed their faith in God that He would make a way beyond animals to cover their sins.

And so Jesus came as the final sacrifice. And in the upper room, He said "this is my blood which is poured out for many for the forgiveness of sins." (Matthew 26:28). Jesus knew His blood was necessary. He knew it had a vital purpose. And while the process was painful and the ultimate separation from the Father was horrific, He willingly walked that path for us.

Apart from Jesus, we would have no path to God. Absent His shed blood on the cross, we would remain guilty, condemned to punishment. Thankfully, He was obedient to death, even to death on a cross. (Philippians 2:8)

We come to this song, not repulsed by the prospect of a fountain of blood, but eternally grateful for it. We know that while blood points to the horror of death, it was a death given on our behalf, payment of the punishment that we should have received.

Joyfully we plunge beneath the crimson flow. Gratefully we accept the payment on our behalf. Humbly we admit that we are unable to do this for ourselves. And we sing this song as a reminder that our salvation did not come cheaply.

No, our salvation and our relationship with God came at a dear price: The death of our beloved Savior. And we claim partnership in that death when we allow His blood to cleanse us from all of our sins.

ROCK OF AGES

Rock of Ages, cleft for me,
Let me hide myself in Thee.
Let the water and the blood,
From Thy wounded side which flowed,
Be of sin a double cure,
Save from wrath and make me pure.

Augustus M. Toplady

Our God is a rock, a solid and secure place to which we can run when the world becomes unstable. In His solid embrace, we can find refuge and security. Deep within a crack seemingly made for us, we can shelter from the storms that rage around us – and find peace.

The hymnist seems to take inspiration from King David.

The LORD is my rock and my fortress and my
deliverer,
my God, my rock, in whom I take refuge,
my shield, and the horn of my salvation, my
stronghold.
Psalm 18:2

David was familiar with hiding among the rocks as he fled from King Saul's wrath. He knew where he could find security, and later in life compared God to those rocks where he found safety.

We are invited to run to the Rock of Ages. God, who is our refuge, invites us to hide in Him. Nothing on earth can shatter or move Him. He is powerful to save us and to keep us from any harm that might threaten us.

This cleft in the rock was made for us by the sacrifice of Jesus. It is precisely His death that opened a place where we can hide. And so we are directed to the water and blood that flowed down His side when He was pierced with the spear. (John 19:34)

From this position of safety and security, nestled in the great Rock of our God, we see our salvation, purchased by the dearest cost of the death of His Son. The benefits of this offering are directed entirely toward us. We cannot add to, or detract from, the price that was paid.

The songwriter calls the cross a double cure, for in that sacrifice we gain two great benefits. We are saved from the wrath of God, which we richly deserve. Our sins cannot be hidden from His ever-present eye. They cannot be justified or explained away. They condemn us as rebels against His law and people who despise their Creator.

"Sinners" seems such a sanitary word to describe who we were. It covers the rebellion and the animosity and the rejection that we directed toward God. In a neat little package, it rolls together our terrible actions and shows us the wrapping paper instead of the ugly contents of our lives.

Yet sinners we were when Christ spilled the water and blood out of His pierced side. His sacrifice took God's just wrath and punishment upon Himself when He had done nothing to deserve it. In this, we are saved from wrath, placed securely in the cleft of the Rock.

But the song continues to describe the second effect of Jesus' death for us. He makes us pure. Certainly, we receive His pure standing before God. But the result of our new relationship and our new heart is that we now desire to be pure like Him.

> And everyone who thus hopes in Him purifies himself
> as He is pure.
> 1 John 3:3

We pursue His likeness, His purity because we now have our hope in Him. He did not pay our price and then leave us to figure out what to do next. He sent His Spirit to indwell us and convict us of sin and intercede on our behalf. He caused us to want to grow up to be like Jesus, exchanging our sinful desires for holy passions.

Secure in the cleft of the rock we can look out at the double benefit of our salvation. Safe from wrath, made pure, and desiring purity for ourselves, we are no longer the same people we were. We have confidence in our Savior and our position before God. We cannot be shaken or torn away from His love and His protection.

ALL HAIL THE POWER OF JESUS' NAME

All hail the power of Jesus' name!
Let angels prostrate fall;
Bring forth the royal diadem,
And crown Him Lord of all;
Bring forth the royal diadem,
And crown Him Lord of all.

Edward Perronet

This song has but one purpose: to lift high the name of Jesus. Its purpose is simply to offer a refrain of praise and make much of who Jesus is and what He has done for us.

The song begins by reflecting that angels must fall at the feet of Jesus. Angels, those spiritual beings whose power is much greater than ours (Psalm 8:5), fall on their faces at the name of Jesus and offer up praise because only He is worthy of their adoration.

We don't think much of falling on our faces in worship today. But this seems to be a common response. Consider John's vision of Jesus upon the throne. The twenty-four elders, each seated on their thrones, fell and lay on the floor and worshipped Him (Revelation 4:9-10). If elders on thrones fall on their faces, how much more so should we, who have no such distinction?

Hail Him, who saves you by His grace,

The second verse commands us to worship Jesus because He purchased our salvation. When we were lost and unable to save ourselves, He came to earth and lived a perfect life but then suffered our punishment (2 Corinthians 5:21). Graciously He extends to us the benefits that He earned in exchange for the condemnation that we deserve.

To Him all majesty ascribe,

The third verse calls upon every person who has lived upon this earth to give all majesty to Jesus. We can hold back no glory for ourselves, for we do not deserve it in the face of His greatness.

Imagine, for a moment, what this would be like. We know what it is like for thousands of people at a sporting event to cheer wildly for their team. The bigger the event, the louder the acclaim. Now begin to multiply that to include every person in your city or town. Instead of thousands of people cheering for a sporting team, imagine millions of people cheering for Jesus! How loud would it be? Could you resist the energy of the cheer and remain unaffected? I don't think so. This would be an irresistible wave of adoration that would catch us up and carry us along.

We'll join the everlasting song,

The final verse brings us to the humble awareness that Jesus' majesty is not a modern phenomenon. For thousands upon thousands of years, Jesus has been worthy of worship. Ever since that first moment, Jesus has been sustaining and holding together the created universe (Hebrews 1:3). Were He to relax for just a moment, all creation could disintegrate back to the nothing from which He called it into existence. Yes, His saving work on the cross was relatively recent. But from the very beginning, from the creation, He has been worthy of worship.

We offer our voices in praise as one refrain of this ongoing song. What we do in our lives here on the Earth is but a prelude, a warm-up, for eternity. When we attain that glorious state, we will see Jesus with our own eyes. We will know His glory in its fullness, and we will join our voices with renewed vigor in that eternal song of praise.

Jesus is worthy of all worship. Every verse of the song ends with one common command: Crown Him Lord of all. Of all. Of everything. He alone is worthy of all glory.

In what areas of your life are you tempted to hold back lordship? How are you tempted to steal His throne and rule on your own? He is far more worthy than you. Don't be a glory thief. Let today be the day you finally surrender to His glory and crown Him Lord of all.

AMAZING GRACE

Amazing grace! How sweet the sound!
That saved a wretch like me!
I once was lost but now am found;
Was blind but now I see.

John Newton

This tune may well be the most recognized of all hymns. It has certainly made its way into our culture. The words are generally well known, even to people who do not understand the full meaning.

The grace of God truly is amazing. In the wide world around us, we will find nothing like it. It is unique, and therefore of incalculable value. Yet God offers it to us freely.

All too often the deep and wonderful meaning of this great hymn is misunderstood or overlooked. What a shame! This song touches on one of the greatest truths of the Bible.

To the believer who understands the grace they have received, "Amazing grace" is a sweet sound. It conjures up images of our Savior on the cross in our place. He suffered and died so that He could offer us the perfect life He lived in exchange for our brokenness and sin. Amazing is too small a word to describe it. Yet it may be the greatest single word that we can apply.

In today's pop-culture environment, no one wants to think of themselves as a wretch. Yet that is what the Bible calls us. Isaiah exclaims that even his most noble deeds, when compared to the glory of God, were like filthy rags (Isaiah 64:6). The Apostle Paul cries out "Wretched man that I am!" (Romans 7:24) We cannot expect to rise above these Bible greats. What holds for them also holds for us.

We are by nature sinners. Not only denied access to God but rebelling against Him and running away from Him. We have no claim on Him or His goodness and mercy. But God shows His love toward in that while we were yet sinners, Christ died for us (Romans 5:8). Mysteriously, inexplicably, when we least deserved it, He saved us from His just wrath.

This salvation completely changes our situation. Before, we were lost. We were unable to find our way to any good destination. We could not get out of the circumstances that gripped us tightly. Yet in Christ, we have been found. God found us, to put a fine point on it. We did not suddenly make a right turn and say "Oh, I know where I am now!" God reached out and drew us to Himself so that we can exclaim "Now I am in Him!"

Before grace, we were blind, ignorant of the spiritual world, and unable to see spiritual truth. In this blindness, we had no way to see the world around us. But, along with being found, we have been given new eyes which allow us to see as we have never seen before. Now we can see what God loves and hates. We can perceive our hearts and motivations. We can understand how we ought to live to please Him.

Amazing grace never grows old. We can sing of it every day and each new dawn find the song as fresh and wonderful as the day before.

When we've been there ten thousand years,
Bright shining as the sun,
We've no less days to sing God's praise,
Than when we've first begun.

The hymnist claims that 10,000 years of praising God for His grace will not drain the tanks of our desire to give thanks and glory to God. Indeed, this is what makes grace so amazing. It never grows old and never fades. Every day we can fall into God's grace and find it just as delightful as the day before.

How Firm a Foundation

How firm a foundation,
Ye saints of the Lord,
Is laid for your faith
In His excellent Word!
What more can He say
Than to you, He hath said,
To you who for refuge
To Jesus have fled?

Rippon's Selection of Hymns

I f you are looking for something strong and stable to build your life upon, look no further than the word of God. You can find no firmer, foundation for your life than the words of life which it contains. When you base your faith upon the truth in your Bible, your life is pointed in the right direction.

This unknown songwriter joins in with King David of ancient Israel, who wrote in Psalm 119:

Oh that my ways may be steadfast
in keeping your statutes!
Then I shall not be put to shame,

having my eyes fixed on all your commandments.
Psalm 119:5-6

The statutes and commandments of God are the firmest foundation we will ever find. And we discover them exclusively in the pages of scripture. People who turn to their Bible find unshakeable truth to guide their life.

Theologians have much to say about the Bible, but none of them say it as beautifully as the songwriter here.

God's word offers the firmest foundation available to humankind. Because God is eternal, so is His word. Because God cannot lie, His word only speaks truth to us. Because God is the creator of everything, His word has the ultimate insight into what is real and how we are made.

The Bible alone provides the full counsel of God. What more can He say? Nothing. Through scripture, He has communicated everything that He wants us to know about Him and about how we ought to live through this Spirit-inspired book. We do not need to keep seeking when we have already found it all. There is no other source of authority that we should listen to. God's word alone is sufficient.

The primary message of the Bible is God's salvation plan. Only because of God's grace displayed toward us can we run to and find refuge in Jesus. The beginning of the Bible points toward the cross. The middle of the Bible tells us of Jesus and His perfect life and perfect sacrifice. The end of the Bible explains how we should live in light of being adopted as children of God.

We have this wonderful gift available to us. We need only open the cover and read the pages to have a delightful conversation with God. If you find yourself reading what sounds like bad news, take comfort for the bad news of sin and condemnation only sets up the good news of forgiveness and everlasting life.

The Bible doesn't pull any punches. It tells real stories of real people. We can identify with them because they are just like us. Moses' bad temper (Numbers 20:11-12), Hannah's desperate prayer (1 Samuel 1:10-18), Peter's foolish babbling (Luke 9:29-35). We find ourselves reflected in its pages, the message of the gospel directed at us.

How often do you turn to your Bible? Is it the first place you turn when you find yourself in troubled times? Or do you forget that you have so mighty a tool at your disposal? When life seems good, do you read about how to live a life that is pleasing to God? Or do you only open it when life seems to turn and crumble?

We are blessed with the full revelation of God's message to us. In it, He has told us about the beginning, the great turning point, and the end. We need no other resource to tell us what we need to do to find Him and live in Him.

Turn to your Bible today. Find comfort in its pages. Meet your Savior and your God and listen to what He has to say.

THERE IS A BALM IN GILEAD

There is a balm in Gilead
To make the wounded whole;
There is a balm in Gilead
To heal the sin-sick soul.
Sometimes I feel discouraged,
And think my work's in vain,
But then the Holy Spirit
Revives my soul again.

Traditional Spiritual

T his song, born of the suffering and toil of slavery, puts its finger beautifully on an experience that still haunts us today. As believers in this sin-infected world, we are subject to hardships and challenges of many sorts. We have not come into our final rest yet. That is still to come.

Meanwhile, we live as aliens in this world. It is not our home or a place of comfort for us. We must find the strength to resist the pain and frustration of our holy desires. We must discover our encouragement from afar because this world will not give it to us.

Gilead is not here. We are not in Gilead. The name points far away to a region of the Holy Land. In the days of King David and Solomon the Wise, Gilead was a region in the Kingdom of Israel. In this way, Gilead today points to a place in the Kingdom of God.

What is this balm? It seems to be spiritual, emotional, and physical. For those who are wounded, the balm brings healing and a restoration of wholeness. For those weary of the tyranny of sin in their lives, the balm brings relief for the soul.

We look forward to God's kingdom, hopefully, expectantly. We cry out to Our Father for relief from the trouble we experience today, knowing that in His presence, such persecution cannot endure. With saints of all ages, we acknowledge that our current troubles are but a bubble compared to the glory that awaits the faithful.

Knowing that Gilead is there and a balm is available should be a great comfort to us. We are not alone, abandoned to our own devices and our efforts. It will not always be as we feel today. We live in the comfort of the promise that we will reign with Jesus in glory.

Yet today we still feel the discouragement and futility of life in this world. We live in a land contaminated by sin and its devastating effects. How then can we bridge the here and now with the promise of the future?

As Jesus promised in John 14, He sends us the Holy Spirit, our Comforter. Straight from the land of Gilead, we have the down payment on our future inheritance. And the Holy Spirit brings comfort and strength to our lives.

When we are discouraged and down, the Holy Spirit reminds us that we are children of the King and circumstances cannot take that Royal decree away from us. When we grow weary of the trouble and problems in this life, the Holy Spirit brings unknown strength to our lives and gives us the power to continue, even when we think we are finished.

This song draws its spiritual inspiration from the prophet Jeremiah. The prophet cried out for the people of Israel, fallen far from God, and in the grip of idolatrous practices. He says that the wounds of his people are like wounds in his own heart. They are wounded and in desperate need of a healer, even if they do not recognize their desperate plight.

> Is there no balm in Gilead?
> Is there no physician there?
> Why then has the health of the daughter of my people
> not been restored?
> Jeremiah 8:22

Jeremiah knew that there was a balm in Gilead. God's love knows no limits, and His forgiveness can restore what has become polluted and broken. Yet for his people, that relief was not to come. Exile was in their future.

For us, however, the balm is available today. We need only cry out to God for strength and courage and He will supply it. As He said to the Apostle Paul "My grace is sufficient for you." (2 Cor. 12:9)

Luxuriate in the balm today. Enjoy its soothing caress. Know that you are not alone with your hardships, but held in the hands of a mighty and loving God.

HOLY, HOLY, HOLY! LORD GOD ALMIGHTY

Holy, holy, holy, Lord God Almighty
Early in the morning our song shall rise to Thee
Holy, holy, holy! Merciful and mighty!
God in three Persons, Blessed Trinity!

Reginald Heber

The triple-holy reminds us of Isaiah's vision of God on the throne in the first three verses of chapter six.

In the year that King Uzziah died, I saw the Lord sitting upon a throne, high and lifted up; and the train of his robe filled the temple. Above Him stood the seraphim. Each had six wings: with two he covered his face, and with two he covered his feet, and with two he flew. And one called to another and said:

"Holy, holy, holy is the LORD of hosts;
the whole earth is full of his glory!"
Isaiah 6:1-3

This song immediately invites us to join with Isaiah before the throne of God. It speaks of God in His holy majesty, for in His holiness, He is exalted above all. There is none like Him. The hymnist reinforces this by naming Him Lord God Almighty. This name sets Him apart from all of creation, for He is the creator, the sovereign ruler over all of His creation.

We respond simply by worshipping Him. Early in the morning implies that upon waking, our orientation is upon God and the first thing we do in our day is to sing a song of adoration to Him. This song is pictured almost like a sacrifice, with the savory aroma of our worship rising to God.

This image of God, holy and mighty, receiving the offering of our worship could be terrifying. Yet the hymn takes a gentler turn by remembering also that God is merciful and mighty. That mercy is turned toward us because it is precisely His mercy that sent Jesus to the cross to pay the price for our sins. This very same mercy offers us the forgiveness of our sins and grants us a position of standing before God as co-heirs with Jesus.

For believers, it is appropriate to sing of our mighty God. We see His power in creation and celebrate Jesus' power in the calming of the storm and the raising of Lazarus. None but a mighty God could apply such power to our broken relationship with Him and bring about a restoration of the relationship that we broke with our sin.

The song concludes by remembering the great mystery of the Trinity. God exists eternally in three Persons, all equal, of the same substance, yet distinct as individual persons but united under one purpose. We cannot fully fathom this. It stretches our mortal understanding to the breaking point. We can only acknowledge that it is true. Someday, perhaps in glory, we will have the capacity to understand this mystery.

This song is critical for us because it reminds us of the glory and majesty of God. He is not of human making. He does not relate casually to us. He is far, far above us. He is Almighty God.

While we might have intimate access and call Him "Abba, Father," we must remember that our daddy created the universe by the sound of His voice and lives in unapproachable light. He is not like a human father, of whom we might have occasion to be ashamed. He is glorious and mighty.

We join with the angels singing "Holy, holy, holy!" We gather before God's throne to worship, early in the morning, before our day begins. We offer the aroma of our praise and adoration to Him, for He alone is worthy.

No matter what happens, if our day is grounded in the worship of a holy God, we can be confident that nothing will befall us of which He is ignorant and nothing will be outside of His power and control. Indeed our God is mighty and not to be trifled with.

Let the holiness of God drift through your mind like an aromatic offering today. Remember who you worship and the mightiness of His name.

BLESSED ASSURANCE

Blessed assurance, Jesus is mine!
Oh, what a foretaste of glory divine!
Heir of salvation, purchase of God,
Born of His Spirit, washed in His blood.

Fanny J. Crosby

W hat greater comfort can we find than the words of this song? What greater truth can we dwell upon than the assurance of our salvation and the blessings that come with our place in Jesus?

Blessed Assurance communicates so much biblical knowledge that a person hardly needs to know more to be considered wise. If only we could live in the confidence of these words, then our lives would be well-centered upon God and our spirits comforted in His care.

The song begins by exulting that "Jesus is mine!" He is my Gift, my Savior, my Shepherd. Indeed, He has given Himself for me and places my welfare above His own. When John records Jesus saying, "For God so loved the world," He meant "For God so loved me."

Perhaps even more true is that I am His. He has purchased me back from slavery and sin. And in His merciful grip, I am secure. We turn again to the gospel of John and his remembrance of Jesus saying,

> "All that the Father gives Me will come to me, and whoever comes to Me I will never cast out."
> John 6:37

Our assurance comes from the strength of His grip. We know that He has overcome death and sin on the cross. The Apostle Paul goes much farther when he writes:

> For I am sure that neither death nor life, nor angels nor rulers, nor things present nor things to come, nor powers, nor height nor depth, nor anything else in all creation, will be able to separate us from the love of God in Christ Jesus our Lord.
> Romans 8:38-39

Blessed assurance. What we have in Jesus now, is just the precursor of many good things to come. We know that He is preparing a dwelling for us (John 14:2) and that we shall be with Him and we shall be like Him (1 John 3:2) in bodies that do not decay or fail and which are cleansed from the taint of sin.

> "What no eye has seen, nor ear heard,
> nor the heart of man imagined,
> what God has prepared for those who love Him"
> 1 Corinthians 2:9

Because of His great sacrifice, we have become heirs of God and co-heirs with Jesus Christ. Stop for a moment and contemplate what that means. Jesus, who is the very expression of perfection, is our co-heir. We are on equal footing and the same terms before God. There is no way that we could earn such a great honor. From our very first effort, we would be disqualified. Yet such is the gift that the very righteousness of Jesus' life is credited to our account, allowing us to stand beside Him as heirs.

As we have been born again of the Spirit, we now have the same Spirit within us. We are no longer estranged and separated from God. He dwells within us, interacting with us, praying for us, prompting and reminding us of what we should do.

The love of God surrounds us and penetrates us, changing us to become more like Jesus. It takes away the heart of stone that was set against God and gives us a heart of flesh that loves God and seeks to please Him. How wonderful that we are not left to our own devices to figure out how to live for God. Our new heart is precisely what we needed to begin this journey of devotion.

Praise God for His blood, shed on the cross. Without that blood, and the sacrifice it represents, we could have no assurance. We would be left to our best efforts, which are wholly inadequate. But Jesus did come and pay the price for our sin, giving us a new life and fresh assurance that we are safe in Him.

I NEED THEE EVERY HOUR

I need thee every hour,
most gracious Lord;
no tender voice like Thine
can peace afford.
I need thee, O I need thee;
every hour I need thee!
O bless me now, my Savior,
I come to thee.

Annie Sherwood Hawks

N o hymn can find a simpler plea than this. "I need you, Lord." This simple cry for God sustains a life lived in devotion to Him.

Crying out for Jesus is the continual need of our lives. On our own, we are often tossed upon life's stormy swells. We have no power to cause the wind and waves to obey us. We may resist the evil one, but we have not overcome him, so his attacks persist.

It is only through the grace of the Lord that we have access to power beyond our own. We gain the protection that is strong to save and mighty to overcome all the forces arrayed against us.

The voice of Jesus in our lives speaks with the tenderness of a parent, soothing our worried souls, imparting confidence that "all will be well." Jesus Himself is the protector of our soul and the Holy Spirit has been sent as the guarantee that our future is secure in Him.

Only through the voice of God in our lives can we find peace. In this sin-scarred world, conflict and striving are the norms. Ever since the curse and the prophecy of Genesis 3, contention has been the rule of the day. And for us, so many years later, the situation has not improved. But God's voice speaks peace into our lives.

As we attend to God, we hear the assurances that we are no longer His enemies. We have been brought close, into His family. He no longer sees us as running away but seeking and desiring Him. In the place of our rebellion and hatred, He sees the blood of Jesus, spilled for us to give us a righteousness we could never earn.

The voice of God also unites us to others throughout the church. We discover that we share a common cause and common love with those who were once strangers to us. As servants are united in the pleasure of their master, we find ourselves coming together to pursue the mission of the Great Commandment (Matthew 22:37-40) and the Great Commission (Matthew 28:19-20).

All these benefits are active while we pursue Jesus. That is when we are attuned to hear the gracious, peaceful, tender voice of God. So let us pursue Jesus more!

It is too little to need Jesus only once per week. Once per day would not suffice either, for too many trials arise throughout the day. So, we call out to Jesus every hour. For every hour challenges come upon us that cause us to call out to Him for fresh love and grace.

The refrain of the song says simply, "I need thee." It is a humble position to acknowledge our need. No false pride can abide where the need is recognized every hour. Crying out for Jesus makes plain the truth about us that we are dependent upon Him. There can be neither shame nor error in admitting that which is true.

This song reminds us of our position in Christ. It does not lay aside the truth of our elevation to children of God. It does not demean the price paid by Jesus on the cross. It simply repeats what is true. In the face of such grace, we still need God. We must heed the words of Jesus:

> Abide in me, and I in you. As the branch cannot bear fruit by itself, unless it abides in the vine, neither can you, unless you abide in me. I am the vine; you are the branches. Whoever abides in Me and I in Him, He it is that bears much fruit, for apart from Me you can do nothing.
> John 15:4-5

We need Jesus. It's a fact. There is neither shame nor dishonour in admitting it. For He is there for us.

MY FAITH LOOKS UP TO THEE

My faith looks up to Thee,
Thou Lamb of Calvary,
Savior Divine!
Now hear me when I pray;
Take all my guilt away.
O let me from this day
Be wholly Thine!

Ray Palmer

Sometimes it is the simplest prayers which are the deepest. We do not need flowery words to express the cry of our hearts. This song is one such prayer. It is simple, yet deep, short yet profound.

As with all wonderful things, we begin by casting the gaze of our faith upon Jesus. Of all the possible viewpoints we could take, the hymnist has selected the Lamb of Calvary as the most pressing perspective. This hearkens back to the introduction given by John the Baptist

The next day he saw Jesus coming toward him, and said, "Behold, the Lamb of God, who takes away the

sin of the world!"
John 1:26

The image of the lamb is inextricably tied to sacrifice in our Bible. To hear Jesus called the "Lamb of God" is a foreshadowing of the sacrifice to come. It's unlikely that John knew exactly what lay in Jesus' future. He would not see that divine payment, but he believed in it all the same.

So the song draws our gaze to the ultimate sacrifice. Jesus went to the cross and died to pay for our sins. For this, He receives the title "Savior Divine." He is Savior, because, through death, He purchased our salvation. He is Divine, because He is God, and lived a perfect life which made it possible for us to receive his righteousness.

The hymn then takes us to prayer. And this is the simplest, purest prayer that we could pray: "Take all my guilt away." It recognizes that we are guilty. As sinners we have fallen short of God's glorious standards (Romans 3:23), and, therefore, stand guilty before our Creator.

It is not a happy thought to think of ourselves as guilty. We tend to justify and explain our behavior. Too often, we compare ourselves to others whom we judge to be "worse" than ourselves. But God does not buy into any of our rhetoric. He sees us measured against His holy standard. And against that rule, He decrees His verdict.

The happiness of this song is that despite our undeniable guilt before God, no matter our powerlessness to do anything about it under our power or action, God extends forgiveness. Not based on any great promises that we make. Not because we have anything valuable to offer in exchange. But solely based upon His love for us.

But God shows his love for us in that while we were
still sinners, Christ died for us.
Romans 5:8)

Forgiveness demands change. We cannot receive so great a
gift and continue as we were before. The hymnist moves
onward to make one final plea for a new life. From this day
forward, so long as we shall live, let us be completely, without
reservation, God's.

This change of ownership rescinds our control over our life.
To be wholly God's means that we have a new allegiance. We
have a new purpose. We have a new agenda. We have a new
power. We have given up our desire to steer our own life and
instead have submitted to God's direction.

This change is not a one-time decision which then carries on
indefinitely. It is a daily decision that we make. Our hearts
are such that, unless we focus continually upon God, we will
revert to our old way of seizing control of ourselves.

Then Jesus told his disciples, "If anyone would come
after me, let him deny himself and take up his cross
and follow me."
Matthew 16:24

Some translations express the phrase "take up his cross" as
"take up his cross daily" indicating that this is not a one-time
decision, but an ongoing decision that we invest in on a daily,
even hourly basis.

"Take away my guilt and make me completely Yours." This is
the prayer of this song, and we do well to remember it and
meditate on it. Ideally, we pray this prayer every day for it
tells the core truth of the gospel.

O WORSHIP THE KING

O worship the King, All glorious above,
And gratefully sing His power and His love.
Our Shield and Defender, the Ancient of Days,
Pavilioned in splendor, and girded with praise.

Robert Grant

T his song stands steadfast through the ages as an eloquent call to worship. After reading the lyrics, how could we not fall to our knees and obey the first line?

Robert Grant took inspiration from Psalm 104 when he wrote this great hymn. This great psalm proclaims God's majesty.

Bless the LORD, O my soul!
O LORD my God, You are very great!
You are clothed with splendor and majesty,
    covering Yourself with light as with a garment,
    stretching out the heavens like a tent.
He lays the beams of his chambers on the waters;
He makes the clouds His chariot;
He rides on the wings of the wind;
He makes His messengers winds,

His ministers a flaming fire.
Psalm 104:1-4

The remainder of the psalm continues to call out God's creation of the Earth: providing clean water for drinking and plants that feed the beasts of the field as well as planting the great forests of cedar, hanging the sun and moon in the sky, and forming the sea upon which ships sail and the leviathan dwells.

The psalmist concludes with this grand statement:

> I will sing to the LORD as long as I live;
> I will sing praise to my God while I have being.
> May my meditation be pleasing to Him,
> for I rejoice in the LORD.
> v33, 34

And so we sing O worship the King. His glory is undeniable. We need only look around us and see the natural beauty He has created to understand that only someone with greater glory than all of creation could make such a thing. Even tarnished and polluted by sin, all of creation stands as a triumphant testimony of the glory of our God.

We gratefully sing of His power and His love, Who so loved us that He sent His Son to earth to do for us what we could not do for ourselves. Our gratitude should know no limits when we consider what He has already done for us. From our position as adopted children, when we look back upon the lives from which we were saved, our automatic response should be to fall to our knees.

But God does not stop there. The hymn goes on to proclaim Him as our Shield and Defender. And indeed, He does intervene on our behalf to protect us from the wicked one. He who has defeated the world comes to our aid when we call upon Him.

God the Father dwells in unapproachable light. He wears Shekinah glory as a robe that no person can look upon lest they are consumed in His holiness. When Moses got a glimpse of just the end of the train of God's robe of glory, he was changed and his face glowed, to the dismay of the people of Israel. And so the hymnist declares He is "Pavilioned in splendor." He who made the beauty of the earth has fashioned for Himself a suitable dwelling that should shout of His greatness.

And so the great hymn comes full circle. After calling us to worship in the first line, we are commanded to praise God in the last. God is girded about with praise. It's like a belt that holds his entire glorious ensemble together. Our voices crying out in delight, admiration, and awe offer the praise that is due. It is not an option or a possibility for us. We must praise God.

Fortunately, because of the greatness of God, this duty is not heavy or onerous. Whenever we think of His creation or His salvation, praise should flow automatically from our lips. Each of us, to the best of our ability, should lift God in worship.

Let today be filled with the adoration of the King.

THE SOLID ROCK

My hope is built on nothing less,
Than Jesus blood and righteousness.
I dare not trust the sweetest frame,
But wholly lean on Jesus' name.
On Christ the solid Rock I stand,
All other ground is sinking sand.
All other ground is sinking sand.

Edward Mote

Let us reflect for a moment on hope. The word is badly misused today. We say things like "I hope it will rain." or "I hope you have a nice day." It has come to mean "wishful thinking." It lacks all confidence and assurance in our modern vocabulary.

That is not how Mr. Mote meant to use it when he penned these words nearly two centuries ago. To him, hope was a powerful concept, grounded in certainty. In this he agrees with the Apostle Peter, who wrote:

> ...but in your hearts honor Christ the Lord as holy,
> always being prepared to make a defense to anyone
> who asks you for a reason for the hope that is in you;
> 1 Peter 3:15

We have hope in us. A hope for peace with God in this lifetime. A hope that all things work together for God's good. Hope for a life after death. I hope for a new body and a continued opportunity to worship God in person.

This hope is not wishful thinking on our part. It is grounded on something very solid - the sacrifice of Jesus Christ on the cross. We get to exchange our sinful rebellion for His righteous obedience. And in that exchange, we are also given new hope.

This hope is a quiet hope. A solid hope. It's not flashy like many of the messages we receive from society today. "Chase pleasure, it will make you feel good," or "The only person you can trust is yourself." These messages come wrapped in fancy paper that looks appealing. The promises are easy and the results seem to be desirable.

Our hope tells us to take up our cross daily and follow Jesus. (Luke 9:23) We are not our own. We have been bought with a price, and we ought to live like it, glorifying God. (1 Corinthians 6:20)

The hymnist's antidote to flashy messages of false hope is to "wholly lean on Jesus' name." This advice is so simple, yet it seems so easy to abandon, precisely because it is so simple.

When we remember what we lean upon, it is much easier to cling to it. Jesus, the One who created and sustains of the universe, (Hebrews 1:3) an equal participant in the fellowship of the Trinity, obedient to the Father's will, set all of His power and prerogatives aside and consented to live the life of His creation. (Philippians 2:5-8) For thirty-three years, He lived a perfect life, maintaining His communion with God. But then He offered up His perfection and His righteousness to die a criminal's death so that we might receive His life credited to our account and be adopted as children of God.

The story of the gospel rests squarely upon Jesus. He is the foundation of our hope. He gives us the confidence to resist the sweet promises of this world that there is a shortcut we can take to get what we want.

This is why the refrain proclaims so boldly that Christ is a solid rock and all other ground, all other promises, are sinking sand. Only in Christ can we find true hope both for today and for eternity. All others will fail us and cause the house of our life to crumble. (Matthew 7:24-27)

We do not place our confidence in a creed or a philosophy but a Person. We trust in the One who loved us so much, He died for us, to purchase us back from sin and death. We rejoice in the Resurrected Savior, who even today sits at the right hand of God advocating for us.

Celebrate your hope in the Solid Rock today. Remember what He has done for you and all the benefits you have already received from Him. Worship Him. Sing His praise. Bless His name. Our hope is built upon Him and we know it is solid.

Just As I Am

Just as I am, without one plea,
But that Thy blood was shed for me,
And that Thou bidst me come to Thee,
O Lamb of God, I come, I come!

Charlotte Elliott

Throughout his crusades, the Rev. Billy Graham used this song as the backdrop to his invitation to come forward and surrender one's life to Jesus. Its message is simple and direct: just come.

For the weary soul, there could be no greater balm than the words "just as I am." All too often we decide in our hearts that we cannot come to God unless we change first. Aware of our sinful state, we might be ashamed of presenting ourselves to the Savior. We might secretly harbor a fear that nobody could love us, and dread the sight of Jesus turning His face away from our disgrace.

Happily, the truth is exactly the opposite. Hanging on the cross, Jesus turned to the thief who hung next to Him and said, "Truly Truly, I say to you, today you will be with Me in Paradise." (Luke 23:43) This man had no opportunity to clean himself up. He hung on the cross of his judgment, condemned to die for his transgressions. He could not have been less presentable to God.

Yet despite his sin and failure, this thief responded to Jesus in faith, and Jesus accepted him. Our thoughts of being able to clean ourselves up fly in the face of this simple profession of faith. God is not waiting for us to become presentable; He is waiting for us to simply turn to Him. He will do the cleaning.

It is precisely because of our spiritual unsuitability that we must come. On our own, we do not have the power to clean ourselves up. Only the shed blood of Jesus Christ can address our filthy spiritual state. Left to our own actions, we only rub more dirt on ourselves. The prophet Isaiah described out best efforts as "a polluted garment." (Isaiah 64:6) Even when we try to act clean under our power, we only become filthier.

On the cross, Jesus gave Himself as the sacrifice to pay the price of our dirty sin. In exchange for covering our sin, He offers us His perfect righteousness. We are allowed to stand before God as if we had lived a life of obedience like Jesus. And we must do... Nothing.

The words "Just as I am" perfectly describe this wonderful exchange. Jesus does not offer limitations on His gift of righteousness. He does not say "this much I will forgive, any more than that you must address on your own." No, His sacrifice is sufficient to cover all our sins and still present us before God as ones who are clean and perfect.

Jesus does not judge us by the dirty lives we bring, but by the faith we lay before Him. It's as if He has already covered us when we come and He sees us through the lens of His blood. We need not feel ashamed of our lives. We should be grateful for the depth of the gift that He freely offers.

How then should we respond to such a wonderful gift? We come. We bring our lives just as they are and cast them upon God's grace poured out so liberally for us. We do not attempt to clean up or defend our sins. We simply present it at the seat of forgiveness and accept the great exchange that Jesus offers.

And so it goes throughout our life with Jesus. He does not judge our sins but stands with open arms ready to forgive them.

> If we confess our sins, He is faithful and just to forgive
> us our sins and to cleanse us from all unrighteousness.
> 1 John 1:9

Just as we are, we need only come.

CROWN HIM WITH MANY CROWNS

Crown Him with many crowns,
The Lamb upon the throne.
Hark! how the heavenly anthem drowns
All music but its own!
Awake my soul and sing,
Of Him who died for thee
And hail Him as thy matchless
King through all eternity.

Matthew Bridges, Godfrey Thring

C rowns signify kingship. To sing a song where every verse begins with the words "Crown Him..." is to sing of the majesty and glory of God. Throughout the hymn, Jesus is lifted as the king, uniquely worthy of worship and glory.

In the first half of this verse, we catch a glimpse of Jesus seated on the throne. We know it is Jesus because He is the only member of the Godhead who is ever described as the Lamb.

These four lines are a compilation of images from the book of Revelation.

His eyes are like a flame of fire, and on his head are
many diadems
Revelation 19:12

This is the picture of Jesus returning with power, at the
Second Coming when He comes as the king instead of a
servant. He is described as a terrible warrior-God and upon
his head are many crowns, signifying that all authority is His.

And between the throne and the four living creatures
and among the elders I saw a Lamb standing, as though
it had been slain.
Revelation 5:6

In this vision, Jesus is pictured as the substitute, who
exchanged His place with ours and now is uniquely qualified
to break the seals of the scroll of inheritance and claim
dominion over all of creation.

And whenever the living creatures give glory and
honor and thanks to Him who is seated on the throne,
who lives forever and ever, the twenty-four elders fall
before Him who is seated on the throne and worship
Him who lives forever and ever.
Revelation 4:9-10

This scene closely parallels that of Isaiah 6. Jesus is seated
upon the throne, with the Seraphim proclaiming "Holy, Holy,
Holy!" all around Him. Yet as these mighty angelic beings
proclaim His holiness, the twenty-four elders fall and sing a
song of worship as well.

This great hymn presents us with Jesus the conquering King,
the suffering Substitute, and the celebrated God. No matter
how we look upon Him, from every angle, He demands our
adoration.

So the hymnist cries out "Awake! my soul!" Wake up! Pay attention. See this Jesus. Don't miss this!

Upon seeing Jesus in all this power and glory, only one response is possible: to join the heavenly anthem of praise. In the presence of so mighty a God, we cannot focus upon ourselves. We must orient our minds and hearts to the One who is worthy of praise. And then sing our hearts out!

We sing a song to which we can deeply relate. Our connection with Jesus is deep and intimate. Our reason for worship is both external and personal. Jesus died for us.

Only through Jesus and His substitution sacrifice do we have access to God. Apart from Him, we are cut off, rebelling against our creator and completely self-absorbed. Only He made a way for us to become children of God and to have a standing in this heavenly realm.

So we must sing. We who have been redeemed and given a new future lift our voices in praise of the One who paid the price of our sin and secured our position before God.

We join with the elders and cast whatever crowns we possess at His feet. Glory does not belong to us; we only seek to reflect the glory that radiates from Him. Only He is worthy of praise, and we will not withhold it.

Consider this song as a mini-vacation to the halls of heaven and the throne of the King. One day we will make this trip in person and participate in the mighty anthem of worship. Until then, let's keep our voices warm and practice crowning Him with many crowns.

WHAT A FRIEND WE HAVE IN JESUS

What a Friend we have in Jesus,
All our sins and griefs to bear!
What a privilege to carry,
Everything to God in prayer!
Oh, what peace we often forfeit,
Oh, what needless pain we bear.
All because we do not carry
Everything to God in prayer!

Joseph M Scriven

P rayer is one of the great benefits of being adopted into the family of God. This hymn places the spotlight directly on the benefits of prayer in the life of the Christian.

Having had our relationship with God changed from rebellious enemy to beloved child, we can now call upon Jesus as our dearest friend. At all times of the day and night, He is never more than a whisper away.

> A man of many companions may come to ruin, but there is a friend who sticks closer than a brother
> Proverbs 18:24

The truth is that we do not stick close to Jesus, He sticks close to us. Our power is weak and fickle. Jesus is strong and constant. We have confidence that when we turn to Him, He will be right there, patiently waiting for us.

As our Friend, Jesus is always glad to hear whatever we want to tell Him. We need not worry that one day He will lose interest in our conversation, or that He will grow weary of the tale of troubles that best us. He knows and understands, for He lived a life just like ours.

> For we do not have a high priest who is unable to sympathize with our weaknesses, but one who in every respect has been tempted as we are, yet without sin.
> Hebrews 4:15

As children of God, we count it a great privilege to have direct access to the Throne of God in prayer. With this access, we can bring every care and concern directly to Him, knowing that He will hear our petitions. We do not have to rely upon a priest or any intermediary to present our requests. No one will filter what we want to ask.

While we come to Almighty God, Creator of the universe with our prayers, He wears the face of Abba Father. We share our concerns and our hopes and make our pleas for strength and help, knowing that He loves us deeply and only wants what is best for us. While that does not guarantee any specific answer we might seek, it ensures that we are given the audience and the chance to ask.

How often do we forget the great privilege of prayer? How many times might we fail to bring our petitions before the throne? Struggling alone in our life, we take on more than we ought because we forget that our Father eagerly waits to hear from us.

> You desire and do not have, so you murder. You covet and cannot obtain, so you fight and quarrel. You do not have, because you do not ask.
> James 4:2

When we decide to pursue our desires, all manner of trouble arises. Our sinful nature rises and twists our life in terrible ways. We exalt ourselves as the provider of good in our own lives. But James says "You have not because you ask not." We forget that we have access to God who can supply all of our needs. (Philippians 4:19)

Turn back to God and exercise your privilege. Remember that through prayer we can entrust our cares, concerns, needs, and wants to our Father who can do so much more than we could even think to ask. He might not answer right away. He might not answer the way we want or expect. But we have confidence that He hears us and brings about good in our lives.

> Now to Him who can do far more abundantly than all that we ask or think, according to the power at work within us, to Him be glory in the church and in Christ Jesus throughout all generations, forever and ever. Amen.
> Ephesians 3:20-21

JESUS LOVES ME

Jesus loves me! this I know,
For the Bible tells me so.
Little ones to Him belong,
They are weak, but He is strong.
Yes, Jesus loves me,
Yes, Jesus loves me,
Yes, Jesus loves me,
The Bible tells me so.

Anna B. Warner

This song is so simple, it might be easier to think of it as a children's song rather than a hymn. While the lyric is written so that children can understand and enjoy, the truth of this song could not be greater.

Jesus loves me is the great truth that rings down through the ages. He began by creating us in His image in the very beginning. (Genesis 1:26) We were created to be loved! His love does not come unexpected or surprising. It is quite natural that we should be the object of His eye.

Yet, despite our favored standing, we sinned. We turned away from God and gave ourselves over to Satan and his rebellious agenda. Our loveable image was marred by the ravages of sin. Rather than being children, we became enemies of God, antagonistic to His involvement and actively running away from His standards.

For many, this seemed like an uncrossable chasm. How could we ever be loved when our trajectory was leading us away from God? Yet God's love was not determined or dictated by our behavior. It has ever been deeply rooted in His character.

> ...but God shows his love for us in that while we were
> still sinners, Christ died for us.
> Romans 5:8

This may be the greatest "But God..." statement in the Bible. While we were dead in our sins, God took action. He did not wait for us to clean ourselves off and become presentable. He did not demand that we get our lives together and meet some minimum standard to prove ourselves love-worthy. He simply loved us and sent His Son to deal with our situation.

We cannot fully comprehend the sacrifice that Jesus made to demonstrate God's love for us. While we might consider our lives here on Earth generally "good," it was an infinite step down for Jesus coming from the glory of heaven. He entered a human body, had to grow up, deal with pain and loss, battle off sickness, and was surrounded every day by sin and its consequences.

Every day of His life, He was tempted to sin, yet every time He refused to give in. (2 Corinthians 5:21) So He experienced the full power of temptation and did not waiver or falter. And because of all of this, He has become our sympathetic representative. (Hebrews 4:15) His sympathy does not alter any standards, but for those who turn to Him, He offers a first-hand understanding of the challenges and trials we face.

Ultimately Jesus demonstrated His love through the cross. He traded His perfect righteousness for our sin - which He had successfully resisted His entire life. He accepted the penalty for that sin, death, and separation from the perfect unity of the trinity.

> Greater love has no one than this that someone lay
> down his life for his friends.
> John 15:13

Jesus spoke these words to His disciples as the end was approaching. He was letting them know that He loved them because He was about to lay down His life for them. We can swap ourselves into that great statement. No greater love will anyone show us than someone lay down His life for us.

The Bible is full of the story of God's love. It tells us how time and time again God's offers of love were mocked, rejected, and wasted by the people to whom He reached out. The story of the Bible is an escalating crescendo to the cross. God's love compelled Him to show His love through Jesus.

We do not need to wonder or be concerned about whether it is true. Simply open your Bible and start reading. God's love will be on every page.

Jesus loves me, this I know!

He Leadeth Me

He leadeth me, O blessed thought!
O words with heavenly comfort fraught!
What e'er I do, where e'er I be,
Still 'tis God's hand that leadeth me.
He leadeth me, He leadeth me,
By His own hand He leadeth me;
His faithful follower I would be,
For by His hand He leadeth me.

Joseph H. Gilmore

What a wonderful testimony! This song brings forth the sheep's quiet confidence in its shepherd.

He leads me in paths of righteousness
for his name's sake.
Psalm 23:3

With Jesus the great Shepherd, we will not want. He loves us and cares for us. He knows exactly what we need and is careful to provide it for us in good time. What a blessed thought, indeed!

When we grow weary, He finds green pastures where we may lie in comfort, surrounded by ample, safe food. He does not lead us into the wilderness and hope we will find comfort there. He takes us to desirable places where our needs can be met. What heavenly comfort is found in this confidence!

Our Shepherd leads us by the still water where we can quench our thirst. He does not take us to the water that we cannot drink. He does not send us out to find our water. He leads us there, knowing that we thirst and exactly what will meet our needs. How blessed it is to have confidence in such a Shepherd who cares for us!

When life turns dark around us, and we walk through the valley feeling death all around, our Shepherd is there with us. He does not fear the things that threaten us. He leads us, bearing His staff with which to both defeat any that would attack and also to draw us back from danger when we stray from the path. It matters not where we may find ourselves, for He is there with us, leading us onward and upward.

He prepares for us a table where we may eat freely and until we are full. We need not fear. He prepares for us a table with foods that are safe for us. He works tirelessly for us, drawing water so that we might drink our fill. He cares for our wounds when we fall or become injured. His attention is upon us and no level of care is beyond His grasp.

With such a shepherd, how can we not feel like kings? How can we not believe that we are in the hand of God? How can we not trust Him?

Where He leads, we follow. We trust Him completely and are content to go where He goes. He has already conquered death and the grave. What could come upon Him that would threaten or harm us?

And so we remain His faithful followers. We go where He leads, confident that His way is the best.

Yet, all we like sheep have gone astray. We need to be reminded of our great Shepherd. We need to return to the 23rd Psalm and this magnificent hymn. In their simplicity, they point us back to our one true love whose care is beyond doubt.

Jesus has already gone to death and back for us. There is no farther He could have gone. There is no greater sacrifice He could make. So we trust Him, knowing that He is the only one who can lead us safely onward.

And when my task on earth is done,
When by Thy grace the vict'ry's won,
E'en death's cold wave I will not flee,
Since God through Jordan leadeth me.

Wherever He leads, we will follow, confident that His judgment is better than ours. We know that He will lead us through any circumstance that may come up. And when all is said and done, He will lead us safely to our heavenly home.

REVIVE US AGAIN

We praise Thee, O God,
For the Son of Thy love;
For Jesus who died
And is now gone above.
Hallelujah! Thine the glory!
Hallelujah! Amen!
Hallelujah! Thine the glory!
Revive us again.

William P. Mackay

T his grand old hymn of the faith blends exultation, beseeching, and the gospel into one melodious whole. It offers a wonderful blend of theology and response that we would do well to embrace in ordinary and challenging days. To meditate upon these words will draw us back to the foot of the cross, the empty grave, and our Savior in glory.

Again and again, our eyes should be drawn back to Jesus who died. More than a simple sentence, it contains an entire world of love and agony. For in that death, Jesus took upon Himself the penalty which we owed for the lives we have lived in rebellion against God. The weight of that penalty was such that the Father, for the first time in all of eternity, turned away His gaze from His beloved Son.

We cannot fathom such a price. We, who have never enjoyed the community of the trinity, cannot imagine what a loss that would have been. Yet Jesus said, "Not my will, but Thine be done." He went to the cross and willingly paid in one moment what would have cost us all eternity apart from God.

But God raised Him on the third day, and He abandoned the grave for a seat at the right hand of God the Father. And there He remains to this day, our Advocate, defending us against the attacks of the devil. He need only point to His hands and feet to thwart the craftiest attack against our security in Him.

> "My sheep hear my voice, and I know them, and they
> follow me. I give them eternal life, and they will never
> perish, and no one will snatch them out of my hand.
> My Father, who has given them to me, is greater than
> all, and no one is able to snatch them out of the Father's
> hand."
> John 10:27-29

In light of such wondrous love and sacrifice, we can only cry out "Hallelujah!" The word literally means Praise ("Hallel" in the original Hebrew) to God (Jah or Yah as in Yahweh). This song itself is an anthem of praise for the goodness of God. It places all glory firmly on God.

In response to the sacrifice, the empty tomb, and the Great Advocate in heaven, the song calls out for a great revival to take place in our lives. "Revive us again." Call us back to life and passion for the Savior who paid our price. Breathe energy into our lives for obedience to the one true God. Give us the will to submit and obey the Spirit who lives within us.

Revive us again;
Fill each heart with Thy love;

May each soul be rekindled
With fire from above.

This is how William Mackay viewed revival. He painted it in the light of Pentecost when the Holy Spirit came down and indwelled the believers and overwhelmed them with the power of God. It was a dramatic, unmistakable, undeniable change. The result cried out for a cause worthy of such an effect, and those around took note of the change in the lives of the original believers.

How is your life today? Could you use a little revival? How about complete revival? Can you sing the words of this great hymn and say "This is what I desperately want in my own life!"?

Consider the words of this song and make your prayer today "Bring revival to my life."

> Will you not revive us again,
> that your people may rejoice in you?
> Psalm 85:6

MY JESUS, I LOVE THEE

My Jesus I love Thee;
I know Thou art mine.
For Thee all the follies
Of sin I resign.
My gracious Redeemer,
My Savior art Thou.
If ever I loved Thee,
My Jesus 'tis now.

William R. Featherson

Have you ever written a love letter to your Savior? Have you set pen to paper or fingers to keyboard and listed out the reasons why you love Him? Have you spoken the words to Him, "I love You"?

This fantastic hymn is a love letter to our Lord. From the first line to the last, it is an unbridled proclamation of love toward Him who first loved us. Read it again, and think of how it lays out the love of the author or a singer.

This is not a courtship letter. It is not written in the hope of developing a relationship. It is not pursuing a love interest. The first sentence states, "I love You because You are mine."

This is a letter written between two lovers, people already in a reciprocated, loving relationship. The letter is itself a celebration of that relationship.

> Repent, therefore, and turn back, that your sins may be blotted out
> Acts 3:19

For the sake of Jesus and our love for Him, we turn away from the follies of our former sinful life. The love of Christ compels us to live differently; not because we want to earn His love, but because we have already received it. The hymn writer calls his sin "folly," that is crazy behavior. It seems good for a moment, but the result is far worse in magnitude than any pleasure. By contrast, the love of Jesus is enduring and brings constant benefit.

> I have blotted out your transgressions like a cloud and your sins like mist;
> return to me, for I have redeemed you.
> Isaiah 44:22

Jesus is our redeemer. He alone is the One who has saved us. Through these actions, Jesus showed His love for us. By offering Himself in our place, He has paid the penalty for our sins. Our price paid, we are purchased from the domain of sin and death into the family of light and life. We who believe have been returned to a right relationship with God, as He intended for us. And we look forward to a future where we shall see Him face to face, as Adam and Eve did in the Garden.

Because we have been redeemed, we can stop striving to find our way to God. No longer do we need to prove our worthiness. We have been given the worthiness of Christ. No longer do we need to strive for perfection. We have been gifted His perfect righteousness. Our redemption greatly exceeds any efforts we could make and gives us the result we so deeply desire.

We love because He first loved us.
1 John 4:19

The hymn concludes each verse with this same statement. If I have ever loved You, Jesus, I love You now. If at any time my love was evident, it is even more so now. Our love grows stronger as time goes by and we rest in the love He first showed us.

There is no action we can take to prove once and for all that we love Him. No such evidence is needed. Our ongoing devotion demonstrates our love far more clearly than any action could. He is not looking for proof of our love, He simply desires our love.

Rest in your love of the Savior. Turn from foolish sins because they are unworthy of His sacrifice. Embrace His payment on your behalf and the truth that He has pulled you out of the miry clay of your previous life. Express your love to Him as the simple fact and reality that it is.

Perhaps you might even try to write your own love letter.

JESUS PAID IT ALL

I hear the Savior say,
"Thy strength indeed is small
Child of weakness watch and pray
Find in Me thine all in all."
Jesus paid it all,
All to Him I owe;
Sin had left a crimson stain,
He washed it white as snow.

Elvina M. Hall

What beautiful words to reflect upon the gospel. Simply put, Jesus paid it all. He didn't make a down payment and leave the ongoing payments to us. He didn't pay the majority and leave a little for us, so we'd have an appreciation of what He had done. He paid it all.

This song brings into clear focus the central truth of the gospel. It is a truth that we need to be reminded of again and again.

For our sake He made Him to be sin who knew no sin, so that in Him we might become the righteousness of

God.
2 Corinthians 5:21

Our flesh is so perverse that unless we return to this truth, it will begin to assume that somehow we are responsible for the benefits of the gospel. Without any real decision on our part, our thinking turns to how good we think we are, and what a benefit that must have been to Jesus on the cross.

It was no benefit. We were no assistance to Jesus as He sacrificed Himself. We were entirely the reason for the sacrifice in the first place.

> For all have sinned and fall short of the glory of God.
> Romans 3:23

We were in the category of "all". There were no special exceptions. There was not a single person in all the history of the earth that could assist Jesus in what He had to do.

So the song opens reflecting upon our weakness. We are completely dependent upon Jesus for our salvation. We have nothing to offer except the reason for the sacrifice in the first place.

Jesus invites us to find everything we need in Him and Him alone.

> Jesus said to him [Thomas], "I am the way, and the
> truth, and the life. No one comes to the Father except
> through me."
> John 14:6

In Jesus, we find the avenue of access to God. Only by faith in the sufficiency of His sacrifice can we approach God. He is the truth. Only through Him can we see ourselves as God sees us. He alone offers eternal life. All other paths ultimately lead to death. And so the hymn writer continues, "Find in Me thine all in all."

Find your life in Jesus. Find your meaning in Jesus. Find your future in Jesus. Find your worth in Jesus.

Jesus paid it all. All to Him we owe. We cannot receive the gift, truly embrace it, and then simply walk away. Such a sacrifice on our behalf creates a debt of love. It changes us and changes our outlook on life. We must admit that only through Jesus does God bless us. Only through Jesus do we receive power.

We need to live more often in the weight of that debt of love. While we are most certainly children of God, we need also to remember that we were gifted that status by Jesus' completed work on the cross. We cannot take credit for any aspect of it. We cannot take for granted that such wealth has been placed at our disposal.

We owe Him everything. We need to remember that and express it back to Him. Not because we're afraid He'll take it all away but because that is the proper reaction to such an extravagant gift.

And when before the throne,
I stand at last complete;
"Jesus died my soul to save,"
My lips shall still repeat.

You don't need to wait for that last moment. You can start singing it today. Jesus paid it all.

SWEET BY AND BY

There's a land that is fairer than day,
And by faith we can see it afar;
For the Father waits over the way,
To prepare us a dwelling place there.
In the sweet by and by
We shall meet on that beautiful shore
In the sweet by and by,
We shall meet on that beautiful shore.

Sanford F. Bennett

This hymn does not delve into deep theological truths but simply reminds us that this world is not our home. It does not represent the best life that we have to live. As believers, we are always oriented to the future because we know it is secured and it will be with Jesus.

When life becomes hard and we are looking for encouragement, we can find joy in this simple truth:

But, as it is written,
"What no eye has seen, nor ear heard,
nor the heart of man imagined,
what God has prepared for those who love Him".
1 Corinthians 2:9

The goodness of God knows no limits. As we look around us, we see His good hand upon our lives. But we know that He has even more goodness in store for that day when we see Jesus face to face. For then this world of sin and death will be set aside and we shall enjoy Him as never before.

The great challenge of the Christian life is balancing the tension between "now" and "then." Now we suffer the fiery darts of the evil one. Now we live in bodies of sinful flesh. Now we are beset by all sorts of troubles that wear us down.

But the day is coming when we shall set all these hindrances aside. For this world is not our final destination and something far greater lies in store for us. We wait expectantly for the time when we shall experience it firsthand. This hope buoys us up as we walk through our lives here on Earth.

Jesus Himself promised that this live we live now would not be the end.

> In my Father's house are many rooms. If it were not so,
> would I have told you that I go to prepare a place for
> you? And if I go and prepare a place for you, I will
> come again and will take you to myself, that where I
> am you may be also.
> John 14:2-3

Jesus is preparing a place for us. This was the promise He made to His closest followers, and it extends to us as well. Even though He ascended to heaven and now sits at the right hand of God Almighty, He has not forgotten us.

And let us not forget that even though He has departed from this Earth, He has sent another Comforter to us, to be with us. We are not alone as we wait for the Sweet By and By. We have the Holy Spirit abiding in us to give us hope and power and remind us of the promise that Jesus made.

Oh, it will be a beautiful shore when we come to that eternal place where Jesus is. Whether through death's portal or via Jesus' return, we will be reunited with Him. It is a glorious future that awaits us there.

We who believe have hope of this future. We count it as certain, even though we have not yet seen it. We dream of what it might be like, knowing that the reality will be so much more.

Take hope and encouragement in the promises of Jesus. Remember that Jesus said that He will never leave nor forsake you. (Hebrews 13:5) Therefore we can be content with our current situation. We have Jesus. And the day is coming when we will see Him with our own eyes.

TAKE MY LIFE AND LET IT BE

Take my life and let it be
Consecrated Lord to Thee.
Take my hands and let them move,
At the impulse of Thy love,
At the impulse of Thy love.

Frances R. Havergal

Of this great hymn of consecration, Frances Havergal once said, "There must be full surrender before there can be full blessedness." She, herself, experienced a moment of clarity around what it meant to surrender her life to Jesus. It became a moment that set her on a path of service to her Savior.

This song, positioned as a request of God, simply asks God to receive our sacrifice. Take my life. Take my hands. God can put them to much better use and effect than we can.

> Whatever you do, work heartily, as for the Lord and
> not for men, knowing that from the Lord you will
> receive the inheritance as your reward. You are serving
> the Lord Christ.
> Colossians 3:23, 24

As redeemed people, we live our lives with a different purpose than those around us. We do not live for ourselves - we have done nothing worthy of our own devotion. We live for our Savior, who has done for us what no other could. He paid the price of our sin and gave us a relationship with God.

Our submission comes from an attitude of love. We love Him because He first loved us. (1 John 4:19). It is not an action or a decision of our choosing. Rather it is something that bursts forth from us because Jesus showed us how much He loved us first. We have been loved. That love changes us, makes us into new people who have different passions and pursuits.

The Apostle Paul summed it up eloquently when he wrote "for me to live is Christ." (Philippians 1:21) The active focus of his life was his Savior. From the day he saw Jesus on the road to Damascus, he was changed. His values, his priorities, his pursuits were all oriented to Jesus.

Take my life and let it be consecrated, Lord to Thee.

Consecrated means set aside for a special purpose. The only worthy purpose would be the mission of Jesus Christ. Any purpose that I could offer would ultimately turn into "dirty rags" (Isaiah 64:6). Serving my purposes is not a path to any great honor to God.

Precious jewelry is not worn to clean the manure out of the barn. Valuable china is reserved for special occasions that it commemorates. In the same way, a life consecrated to Jesus cannot also be used for our purposes. We dirty that life; we contaminate it with worthless activity.

> I have been crucified with Christ. It is no longer I who live, but Christ who lives in me. And the life I now live in the flesh I live by faith in the Son of God, who loved me and gave Himself for me.
> Galatians 2:20

We are to take up our cross daily and consider ourselves crucified. Our wants and desires need to hang on that cross so that we can move beyond them and see the life of Jesus instead. He has purchased our lives through His death, and so it is proper that we should live them for Him.

This great hymn does not stop at our lives and our hands. It continues to consecrate our feet, asking that they be swift and beautiful to Jesus, echoing Romans 10:15 "How beautiful are the feet of those who preach the good news!" Our feet, which take us out into the world, should be surrendered to Jesus to be the vehicles of the gospel for those who do not know Him.

Take my lips and let them be filled with messages for thee. James says that the hardest part of our body to tame is the tongue. Yet this hymn calls for Jesus to take our lips and the words that we speak. May they be dedicated to speaking of Jesus. Any lesser words coming from our mouths pollute the sacrifice which He made to redeem all of us. If Christ has redeemed us, then let our mouths be first of the redemption.

Take my love. If there is any part of us that the song has not specifically called out, it is covered under the final stanza. Our love, the outpouring of our lives, touches everything about is. Let our own lives be suppressed and replaced with an overwhelming love of Christ. Let all of our energy be directed to Him who gave Himself for us.

Take my life and let it be consecrated, Lord to Thee.

IT IS WELL WITH MY SOUL

When peace like a river,
Attendeth my way,
When sorrows like sea billows roll,
Whatever my lot,
Thou hast taught me to say,
"It is well,
It is well, with my soul."
It is well, with my soul.
It is well,
It is well with my soul.

Horatio G. Spafford

For many, the story of this song is familiar. In 1873, Horatio Spafford sent his family to England by ship. He had hoped to spend time with Dwight Moody and Ira Sankey at an evangelistic rally. The ship collided with another boat and sank, drowning his four daughters. His wife, saved by a sailor, sent him a terse telegram from London: 'Saved Alone.' Horatio set sail to reunite with her, and by agreement with the captain was awakened one night as the ship passed the watery grave of his daughters.

He wrote these words.

At a time when life seems dark, when it seems like the evil one is having his way when our emotions are broken and our hopes are dashed, that is when we need these words: "It is well with my soul."

Jesus Himself promised us that our lives would have hardship and trouble. Rather than thinking that a Christian life will prevent troubles, we need only listen to the words of Jesus.

> "I have said these things to you, that in Me you may
> have peace. In the world, you will have tribulation. But
> take heart; I have overcome the world."
> John 16:33

In this world, we will have tribulation. Whether it be spiritual persecution or the normal turns of human life. We should not be surprised when it shows on our doorstep. Jesus told us it was coming.

At the same time, He offers us an even better reminder. He has overcome the world. The principalities and powers that Paul describes in Ephesians 6 have been defeated. They cannot overcome Jesus.

In Hebrews 13:5 we are reminded that Jesus said "I will never leave you nor forsake you." We don't have to bear these troubles and tribulations alone. Jesus, the conqueror, is with us and will ensure that whatever we may experience, we will come out on the other side secure in His love.

Whatever my lot, Thou hast taught me to say "It is well with my soul".

Have you learned to say this? For Horatio G. Spafford, that moment on the ship was the culmination of a lifetime of lessons leading to his ability to pen this encouraging reminder.

Resting in Jesus is not something that comes automatically just because we've said a prayer somewhere along the way. It comes by saying "It is well with my soul" when small things go against us. These are moments of practice. Just like any physical activity, the easy work in the early days builds our strength so that when the hard work comes, we are prepared and ready.

"It is well with my soul" means that while we may not like the circumstances, we accept that God is in control and this is somehow part of His good plan. While we may not understand it at the moment, we are grounded in the truth that God is sovereign. No matter how out of control the situation feels to us, God has it well under control.

"It is well with my soul" does not mean that we're always happy. When the details seem dark, it means that we cling even more tenaciously to the truth of who we are in Jesus. It means that we acknowledge what has happened is something that Jesus has allowed into our lives. And regardless of the emotion, we feel, He understands exactly what we're going through.

We don't know the outcome of any situation against an eternal background. Perhaps from the perspective of glory, we'll be able to see these circumstances from God's vantage point. Until then, our response is to say, "It is well with my soul" and rely upon Jesus.

ALL THE WAY MY SAVIOR LEADS ME

All the way my Savior leads me;
What have I to ask beside?
Can I doubt His tender mercy,
Who thro' life has been my guide?
Heav'nly peace, divinest comfort,
Here by faith in Him to dwell!
For I know what e'er befall me,
Jesus doeth all things well.

Fanny J. Crosby

When we look back on our lives, it is easy to ask "What if?..." What if we had made a different decision? What if we had stopped and waited? What if we had listened to advice?

There is one thing we cannot question, however. We cannot question Jesus and His care for us. We cannot second guess Him. We cannot doubt His love or affection for us.

All the way that He has led us through this life, whether it is fifty years or five days, we know that there is nothing more we could ask of Him. His goodness is above reproach. His tender mercy is beyond dispute. His wisdom is undeniable.

What more could we ask of Jesus? Was it not enough that He went to the cross in our place? Can we ask for more than His payment of our debt? Can we demand more than His death for our sins and that we received in return His righteousness and His perfect life?

There is a friend that sticks closer than a brother (Proverbs 18:24). Our Jesus is so close He stood in our place. He could not have come any closer. No relative could ever do what He has done.

Spiritual peace is ours because of Jesus. Before Him we were enemies of God, running away in rebellion as fast as we could. Jesus arrested our flight and set us before the throne, not as rebels, but as sons and daughters. Comfort is ours because Jesus has brought to us the Great Comforter in the Holy Spirit.

How could we be unhappy with the course of our lives in Jesus? What basis do we have to compare? There is no greater love that He has shown us. How could such love do ill to us? It can't.

Fanny Crosby lived a hard life. Blind as a young girl, she never had the opportunity to see the beauty in the world around her. Yet she saw Jesus. And in Him, she saw all the beauty that she needed. Her world was shaped and dominated by Jesus, and as she concluded in the hymn, Jesus does all things well.

Let this be an encouragement to us. Jesus has not stopped doing all things well. His love and care for us have been done to the best of standards. The future He has prepared for us is beyond what our eyes have seen and our hearts have heard. The gifts He has given us are not gag gifts, but the things we need more desperately than anything in our lives: Hope, Love, and Faith.

All the way our Savior leads us, we have no reason to complain because He does everything well.

Yes, the world hates us just as it hated Him. We may be persecuted and reviled because of our faith in Him. But He has overcome the world (John 16:33). It has no power to do anything which He does not permit. The grave and death hold no terror for us because we know that to be absent from this body is to be present with Him. (2 Corinthians 5:8)

When Jesus calls us to follow Him, we dare not refuse. In Him is life and all that is good. On our own, we could not hope to assemble as much good as He offers us freely. We turn to Him and gladly go where He leads because we know that He will guide us safely home and that in His hands we are safe from all attackers.

LIKE A RIVER GLORIOUS

Like a river glorious, is God's perfect peace.
Over all victorious, in its bright increase;
Perfect, yet it floweth, fuller every day,
Perfect, yet it groweth, deeper all the way.
Stayed upon Jehovah, hearts are fully blest
Finding, as He promised, perfect peace and rest.

Frances R. Havergal

What grander topic could we consider than the peace of God? For a people who come into this world at war with Him, the prospect of peace with Him and His peace in us is such a far cry from any reasonable expectation we could hold. Yet through Christ Jesus, such peace is ours.

> Therefore, since we have been justified by faith, we
> have peace with God through our Lord Jesus Christ.
> Romans 5:1

As amazing as it sounds, we, who rebel against God have found a way to experience peace with Him through our Lord Jesus Christ. Who could have expected that God Himself would sign the peace treaty and seal it with the blood of His own Son? Yet that is exactly what has happened.

In one move, by placing our trust in Jesus, we have been converted from enemies to sons and daughters. We are members of His family, seated with Him in the heavenly places. All traces of our rebellion have been separated from us as far as the east is from the west.

This peace with God rolls over us like a river, unstoppable in its force. We need do nothing more than accept it. We cannot add to it or enhance it. The perfection of this peace is obtained by and guaranteed by God.

But He goes beyond peace with God and offers us the peace of God.

> "Peace I leave with you; my peace I give to you. Not as the world gives do I give to you. Let not your hearts be troubled, neither let them be afraid."
> John 14:27

Jesus leaves us with the peace of God. Not a worldly peace, not a temporary peace, not a partial peace. He leaves us with peace that means our hearts should not be troubled.

He said these words to His disciples when He let them know He would be leaving them. They could not have considered a more terrifying prospect. Having stirred up the animosity of the religious leaders, He was the only buffer preventing them from being overrun by persecution.

Yet Jesus said that His peace was sufficient to calm even that overwhelming fear. Their hearts did not need to be troubled by the prospect of His departure. The peace He was about to leave them would be more than adequate for the challenges they would face.

Humanly, it's tempting to say "We can't imagine anything being stronger than Jesus' presence." Yet Jesus said His peace was enough to handle whatever would come. And as we look at the history of the church, Jesus was right. His peace was sufficient to carry forward His mission here on earth. Emboldened by the Spirit, the early church turned the world upside down in a way that no army could.

> Another time, Jesus said "I have said these things to you, that in Me you may have peace. In the world, you will have tribulation. But take heart; I have overcome the world."
> John 16:33

He has overcome the world. That means it cannot do anything to us that is bigger or stronger or more terrible than what He will allow. He has it on a leash. He is in control. Because of this, He has the power to offer us peace.

Peace does not necessarily mean the absence of hard times. Jesus promises us tribulation. But His peace is deeper and more swiftly flowing than any hardship could ever be. If we take our eyes off the waves around us and focus on Jesus, we will allow His peace to work in us.

Like a river glorious, is God's perfect peace.

TAKE TIME TO BE HOLY

Take time to be holy,
Speak oft with thy Lord;
Abide in Him always,
And feed on His word.
Make friends with God's children,
Help those who are weak.
Forgetting in nothing,
His blessing to seek.

William D. Longstaff

T his great hymn outlines the path to personal holiness through the classic practices and disciplines of the Christian faith. If we wanted a roadmap to point the way and outline the path, this song speaks to the plan that we should follow.

This hymn was inspired by the divine command "You shall be holy, for I am holy." (1 Peter 1:16) How then shall we be holy? We certainly cannot do it by force of will alone. Holiness is the product of righteous living. So we should focus on the activities of righteousness to discover holiness.

"Speak oft with thy Lord." Prayer is an easy practice when we find ourselves in need. It is our natural inclination to cry out for help when we are in times of trouble. But the holy practice of the righteous life is to pray in times of need and in times of plenty. Paul commanded the Thessalonians to pray all the time. He knew that spending time communicating with God would produce great effects that went beyond the simple act of prayer itself.

Pray without ceasing.
1 Thessalonians 5:17

"Abide in Him always." To abide means to stay connected; to continue to believe and exercise faith. It might be hard to imagine how we do this, but if we keep Jesus top of mind, always close at hand, we will abide in Him. Day in and day out, being mindful of the gospel keeps us connected to the truth of who we are. Jesus encouraged His disciples to stay the course and not abandon their faith and hope in Him.

"Whoever abides in Me and I in him, he it is that bears much fruit, for apart from Me you can do nothing."
John 15:5

"Feed on His word." No source of encouragement and hope can top our Bibles. We need to daily read what God has said to us. No other truth will shape and give purpose to our lives. No other authority has the answers that we so desperately need. God's word connects us to Him. It was written for us to know Him, and only has power in our lives when we read what He has to say to us.

Your word is a lamp to my feet and a light to my path.
Psalm 119:105

"Make friends with God's children." Christianity is not intended to be a solo venture. We need each other to encourage and strengthen and teach one another. We give comfort and help and even hope to each other in a way that is designed to draw us closer to God, together. Paul, when trying to describe the church, used the idea of a body with many parts. None of the parts function in isolation. They all rely upon the rest of the body for support. The end goal, of course, is building up the entire body and causing it to more closely resemble Jesus.

> Not neglecting to meet together, as is the habit of some,
> but encouraging one another, and all the more as you
> see the Day drawing near.
> Hebrews 10:25

"Help those who are weak." We were weak when Jesus helped us. We were unable to save ourselves when He sacrificed Himself. Therefore, we are to carry this same selfless love to those around us. It matters not if they are a popular friend or an unsavory neighbor. The love of Christ constrains us and compels us to show love, especially when it is unearned and undeserved.

> Religion that is pure and undefiled before God, the
> Father, is this: to visit orphans and widows in their
> affliction and to keep oneself unstained from the world.
> James 1:27

Remember this song. Let it shape and guide your devotion to your Lord today.

'TIS SO SWEET TO TRUST IN JESUS

'Tis so sweet to trust in Jesus,
Just to take Him at His word;
Just to rest upon His promise;
Just to know "Thus sayeth the Lord."
Jesus, Jesus how I trust Him!
How I've proved Him o'er and o'er!
Jesus, Jesus, precious Jesus!
O for grace to trust Him more!

Louisa M. R. Stead

This great hymn could easily become the grand anthem of all Christianity. As people redeemed and saved by the completed work of Jesus at the cross, we have become the people who trust in Jesus. These words bring into sharp focus the joy and benefit of this trust.

We take Jesus at His word and trust in what He has said. When He cried out on the cross "It is finished!" we take it for truth and trust that our salvation is an accomplished fact. When He told his followers "My yoke is easy and My burden is light," (Matthew 11:30) we come alongside Him and happily labor with Him.

The gospel changes everything, and Jesus is the center of the gospel. So we orient our lives around Him and celebrate what He has done for us. Even though we cannot see Him or the things He has done, we experience them in our lives, and in our spirit, we rejoice.

The core of our trust is that we rest in His promises. We can do nothing to make the promises more or less effective. By our efforts, we cannot make a single promise more likely. Our only option is to step aside and let Him do the work.

And oh, His promises are so fantastic! Who would not want to rest in them?

> All that the Father gives Me will come to me, and
> whoever comes to Me I will never cast out.
> John 6:37

> I give them eternal life, and they will never perish, and
> no one will snatch them out of my hand.
> John 10:28

> I have said these things to you, that in Me you may
> have peace. In the world, you will have tribulation. But
> take heart; I have overcome the world."
> John 16:33

> In my Father's house are many rooms. If it were not so,
> would I have told you that I go to prepare a place for
> you? And if I go and prepare a place for you, I will
> come again and will take you to myself, that where I
> am you may be also.
> John 14:2-3

Knowing that Jesus said these things brings great comfort. He accepts all who come to Him, regardless of their resume or rap sheet. He is strong enough to hold them against all comers nor can anyone snatch us from His mighty nail-scarred hands. Even though we will have tribulation in our lives, we can rest in the truth that Jesus has already overcome the world that presses in upon us so heavily. And when all is said and done, we have a future with Jesus in heaven.

It is sweet to trust in Jesus. Again and again, He has proven Himself worthy of our trust. When we trust in Him, He will not let us down. As we look back across our lives, we can see the examples of His faithfulness and love. When times are difficult, these memories become our treasure. They remind us of His character and His promises that always come true and reign in our lives.

The hymn ends with the phrase "O for grace to trust Him more!" How much can we say that, even today? O that we would increase our trust in Jesus! He has done everything necessary for us to trust Him. It only remains for us to lean into that trust and celebrate Him as our all in all.

HOW GREAT THOU ART

O Lord my God,
When I in awesome wonder,
Consider all the worlds Thy hands have made;
I see the stars,
I hear the rolling thunder,
Thy pow'r throughout the universe displayed.
Then sings my soul,
My Savior God, to Thee,
How great Thou art! How great Thou art!
Then sings my soul,
My Savior God, to Thee,
How great Thou art! How great Thou art!

Carl Boberg

H ave you ever gone far away from the city lights and looked up at the night sky? It's filled with stars. The Milky Way traces a path across the heavens so thick you might think you could walk on it. It's enough to make a person feel small.

And God made the two great lights - the greater light to rule the day and the lesser light to rule the night - and the stars. And God set them in the expanse of the

heavens to give light on the earth, to rule over the day and over the night, and to separate the light from the darkness. And God saw that it was good.
Genesis 1:16-18

God made all of that. He spoke, and they came into existence. Their distance was no problem for Him. Their overall size caused Him no difficulty. And we know today that there are millions of stars that we can't see with our eyes alone.

When we look into the sky and think it is majestic and beautiful, that's just a fraction of what God is. He imagined the night sky even before the first star appeared. He placed each star exactly where He wanted it. And then He just made it all.

We are left to wonder and exclaim, "God, You are great!"

This same amazement repeats for the ocean, waterfalls, sunsets and sunrises, mountains, flowers, thunder, and lightning - just about any element of nature that we can see. When we slow down enough, we notice how wonderful it all is. And every bit of it is part of God's great creation.

A God who could make such a delightful world has to be wonderful Himself. What He created, what we see, can only be a reflection of who, and what, He is.

This great hymn captures so much of the wonder we feel in nature. But we can't deny the reality that regardless of how delightful that is, God is even greater. This hymn reminds us of where our true adoration belongs. It's tempting to be caught up in creation and make it the object of our attention. But we must look beyond creation to the Creator.

In the chorus, the greatest wonder of all is referenced. God is not called "Creator God", He is called "Savior God". God's most magnificent work did not occur in Genesis. We read about it in the gospels.

Jesus came to the world that He created. Every night He looked up at the stars that He made and every morning He watched the sunrise. He lived in the dust and the grime of this world, He laughed, He cried, He had friends. But mostly He lived perfectly and did not sin. Not once.

Then, in the prime of His human life, He allowed sinful humans to nail Him to a tree that He created and He died, paying for the sins of everyone who believes in Him.

This is truly amazing. I don't want to take away from the wonder of the starry night sky. But the act of salvation transcends every natural wonder we could ever see.

If we cry out "how great Thou art!" when we see the wonders of nature, how much more so when we consider our salvation that cost the life of the God who created nature?

The next time you see an spectacular view of the natural world, stop and enjoy it. Then think about how much greater is Jesus sacrifice for you.

TRUST AND OBEY

When we walk with the Lord
In the light of His Word,
What a glory He sheds on our way!
While we do His good will,
He abides with us still,
And with all who will
Trust and obey.
Trust and obey,
For there's no other way
To be happy in Jesus,
But to trust and obey

John H Sammis

I f spiritual growth is our aim, then we would do well to follow the instruction of this great hymn. Written in the throes of D. L. Moody's revival movement, this song boils down to a single statement the entirety of the Christian life in a simplicity seldom rivalled.

The title and the chorus rest on the core truth of the song: Trust and obey. This is the only way. It is the way to contentment. It is the way to satisfaction. It is the way to significance. It is the way to be happy in Jesus.

Trust in the LORD with all your heart,
  and do not lean on your own understanding.
In all your ways acknowledge Him,
  and He will make straight your paths
Proverbs 3:5-6

The writer of the proverbs, the wisest man who ever walked the earth, King Solomon, gives the same command. Trust in the Lord. In truth, it is our only option. We know all too well the disappointment and pain that comes from trusting in ourselves. We fail. We are overcome by circumstances. We lack knowledge and power. All reliance upon ourselves is sheer folly.

We trust in the Lord for our salvation. From the beginning, it has always been so. Faith is simply trusting that something is true, without evidence, based solely on the character of the One who said it. We trust in God, He is faithful to forgive us. (1 John 1:9)

We trust in the Lord for our daily sustenance. We trust in His promises. He will never leave us nor forsake us. He is the friend that sticks closer than a brother. He has gone to prepare a place for us, so that we may be with Him forever. In this life, we will face trouble, but He has overcome the world. We will not be tempted beyond what we can withstand.

Our trust in God is multi-faceted. It is a characteristic and hallmark of the Christian faith. How often do we think about our trust? How often do we remark that we live by trusting God daily? Are we aware of the layers of active trust which guide our daily life? What would it look like to make our trust in God explicit? A journal? A prayer diary? Perhaps we should consider such tools to bring us back to the basics of our Christian life.

But trust alone is not enough. We must also obey.

"Has the LORD as great delight in burnt offerings and sacrifices,
  as in obeying the voice of the LORD?
Behold, to obey is better than sacrifice,
  and to listen than the fat of rams."
1 Samuel 15:22

Obedience is trust in action. When we obey, we give legs and arms to our trust. In his letter, James the brother of Jesus wrote "Faith without works is dead." In other words, trust without obedience is ineffective. Or perhaps, trust without obedience is invisible and has no effect.

Talk is cheap. Actions matter. Through our obedience, we declare our trust in God. If we believe what He says, then we will act and behave correspondingly. So let's take some time to do a "Trust Check". How much do we trust? How does that trust express itself in obedience? Where are we disobedient and therefore not trusting?

If you want happiness in this life, there is only one path. Trusting and obeying Jesus. You were made for this. It is the full expression of who you were created to be. Once Jesus reaches out to you, your only path to happiness is through His embrace.

Dedicate yourself to obeying Jesus today. Consider where your trust is weak and offer it up to Him in prayer. Ask Him to give you both greater trust and the strength to obey.

MY FAITH HAS FOUND A RESTING PLACE

My faith has found a resting place,
Not in device or creed;
I trust the Everliving One,
His wounds for me shall plead.
I need no other argument,
I need no other plea,
It is enough that Jesus died,
And that He died for me.

Lidie H. Edmunds

How wonderful it is to find a resting place. In this world, we strive for so many things. It becomes a precious joy when at last we can lay down our efforts.

For many of us, rest comes all too seldom. We trudge onward, carrying our burdens, pressing toward whatever goals we might desire. But in this hymn, we are invited to rest.

Our rest is found in the person of the Lord Jesus Christ. In Him, we place our faith, and then we lay down our burdens and rest (Matthew 11:30). This is a great resting place. From this eternal rest come all other forms of rest that we might enjoy.

The foundation of our rest is indeed our faith in Jesus' once-for-all sacrifice. He paid the full price of our rebellion and our sin. He went to the cross and gave His life, breaking, for the first time, His communion with the unity of the Godhead. Alone, He suffered and bled and died. When He uttered the words "It is finished" upon the cross, He meant that the work of redemption was complete.

Because of Jesus' sacrifice, our faith has found its resting place. The complete payment has been made and needs no other effort from us. We do not need to "clean up our act" or behave in a certain way to earn favor from God. Jesus did not bring us to the door of salvation and require us to fight our way across. God didn't cover eighty percent of the task, leaving the last twenty percent to us. Jesus' work on the cross satisfied all of God's just demands and purchased the entirety of salvation for us.

Because of His work, we can rest. We can say "I am a child of God because of Jesus." He has done everything. He simply asks us to receive His gift. As the song says, "His wounds for me shall plead." Whenever we doubt, look to Jesus on the cross. Whenever we experience temptation, look at the blood He shed for us. Whenever we fail for the hundredth time, look at His body broken, bearing the punishment we deserve.

The chorus of this song rings triumphant: I need no other argument! The case has been settled. It doesn't need a cherry on top "just in case." It is finished.

Our Advocate, who pleads on our behalf, (1 John 2:1) has delivered an unbeatable argument. There is no charge or accusation which can be brought against us that He has not already defeated. We do not need to worry about what the Judge will say, the outcome is guaranteed, because everything the law demanded has been satisfied.

So we are free to rest. We do not need to seek out the perfect trick or gimmick. We do not need to find any additional insurance. We do not need to try to find a better defense from somewhere else in the Bible. We are free to rest.

Sometimes we do not know how to rest. Striving is a natural human tendency. Even though the case is closed, we press onward anyway because we don't know how to do anything else. Even then, this great hymn speaks to us, telling us that we should stop all our work and simply let Jesus' sacrifice be enough. We can't make it any better than it already is.

Let the lyric and the tune of this grand song of the faith remind us to rest. Let it point us to the cross where Jesus' precious blood did what we could never do ourselves. Let it strengthen our faith that Jesus is enough.

WHEN THE ROLL IS CALLED UP YONDER

When the trumpet of the Lord shall sound, and time shall be
no more,
And the morning breaks eternal bright and fair.
When the saints on earth shall gather over on the other shore,
And the roll is called up yonder I'll be there.
When the roll is called up yonder,
When the roll is called up yonder,
When the roll is called up yonder,
When the roll is called up yonder I'll be there.

James M. Black

E very day we wake and go about our business, just the same as the day before. Day after day, the same pattern plays out across our lives. It is so tempting to be lulled into thinking that everything we have experienced is everything we ever will experience.

This great hymn is a reminder that our life here on earth is but a short time. Whether by death or by the return of Jesus, our greater destiny awaits us. Our goal will not be to show up in our lives but to answer the roll call in heaven.

The Apostle Paul, writing to the church in Thessaloniki, faced a similar problem. They worried that this life was everything and those who died were going to miss out on all the joy when Jesus returned. Trying to shift their attention, under this inspiration he wrote of something he had never seen, but which he knew to be true.

> For the Lord, Himself will descend from heaven with a cry of command, with the voice of an archangel, and with the sound of the trumpet of God. And the dead in Christ will rise first. Then we who are alive, who are left, will be caught up together with them in the clouds to meet the Lord in the air, and so we will always be with the Lord.
> 1 Thessalonians 4:16, 17

It is not going to be like yesterday forever. The trumpet will blow and Jesus will return and we will be ushered into a new reality where we are with Him.

Gone will be the daily grind of work or school. We will have new tasks and responsibilities, not the least of which will be to worship and praise His name forever.

We can take comfort in the gathering of the saints "over on the other shore" if our confidence is in Jesus. If we are relying upon His sacrifice to be the complete payment of our sin-debt, then we can have confidence that one day, we will answer that heavenly roll call.

> Believe in God; believe also in me. In my Father's house are many rooms. If it were not so, would I have told you that I go to prepare a place for you? And if I go and prepare a place for you, I will come again and will take you to myself, that where I am you may be also.
> John 14:1-3

Jesus, Himself has promised to prepare our place. Just as He has written our names on the eternal roll, He is preparing a place for us (John 14:6). We can have confidence that this life is not all that living has to offer, for when we reach heaven - however, we get there - we will be expected.

Let this be an encouragement for us to shift our focus away from our daily routine. The day is coming when we will no longer trudge along this mortal life. We shall rest in heaven, answering that roll call along with all the saints, casting our crowns at the feet of Jesus.

While we live here on earth, our hope is in the heavenly places where Jesus waits for us. And in His time, He will come again and end this life that we know and call us to be with Him forever.

AT CALVARY

Years I spent in vanity and pride,
Caring not my Lord was crucified,
Knowing not it was for me He died
On Calvary
Mercy there was great and grace was free;
Pardon there was multiplied to me;
There my burdened soul found liberty,
At Calvary.

William R. Newell

Т his great hymn tells the salvation story of the lyricist, William Newell. The first verse describes his broken and sinful condition that cried out for a savior. Even though he did not know or care about the salvation story, he needed to be saved.

The nature of the gospel is such that this song could be sung of anyone. It is not exclusive to Mr. Newell. It is our story too.

We all began in rebellion against God. Children of Adam, we shared in his rejection of God and the pursuit of his way. We validated Adam's decision in our own life by choosing to sit on the throne of our own life and call our shots. Vanity and pride were the least of the sins we committed. Glory thieves, liars, and narcissists, we rejected God even as we knew we were short of the goal.

The second verse describes the moment of conversion and the third verse tells of the life lived for the love of God. But the chorus focuses in on what God was doing. Mercy, grace, and pardon were all found in abundance at Calvary.

Mercy focuses on not getting what we deserve. Our lives deserved justice and punishment. Were it not for the application of mercy in our lives, we would receive the wrath of God for our sins.

> [But] God, being rich in mercy, because of the great
> love with which He loved us, even when we were dead
> in our trespasses, made us alive together with Christ
> Ephesians 2:4, 5

Grace focuses on getting something that we have not earned. To say "grace is a gift" is to be redundant and repetitious. We have received so many things that we do not deserve. Our position as children of God, an inheritance alongside Jesus, the power of the Holy Spirit in our lives.

> For by grace you have been saved through faith. And
> this is not your own doing; it is the gift of God.
> Ephesians 2:8

To be pardoned is a legal status. It means that even though one is guilty of the offense, the punishment is set aside. As sinners, we are all guilty of sinning against God. Only because God, as the Judge, has pardoned us can we find ourselves in a happy relationship with Him.

This hymn of the faith draws us back to Calvary. It reminds us of who we were before we were changed by Jesus' sacrifice.

It drives home the reality that we did not accomplish anything on our own, but all of the work was done by Jesus living a life that completely satisfied God's holy demands - then at the last moment, He traded His perfect life for our punishment.

We do well to remember that we have been the recipients of amazing and boundless mercy, grace, and pardon. Should we forget this, we run the risk of allowing that same vanity and pride to enter back into our lives and taint that relationship which was purchased for such a dear price.

Calvary stands as a reminder to us of who we were - in stark contrast to what we have been declared to be. The last stanza captures it so well:

O the love that drew salvation's plan!
O the grace that brought it down to man!
O the mighty gulf that God did span.
At Calvary!

I SURRENDER ALL

All to Jesus I surrender,
All to Him I freely give;
I will ever love and trust Him,
In His presence daily live.
I surrender all,
I surrender all.
All to Thee my blessed Savior,
I surrender all.

Judson W. Van De Venter

This song is composed of simple words, yet they express a profound truth. Only in surrendering do we find peace. Only by giving up can we gain so much.

The song boldly declares "I surrender all". This inspirational statement generally does not find long-term roots in our lives. Because of our sinful nature, it is natural for us to give away in surrender, then to decide we were fine before and take it back. The process of surrender is not a one-time event, but an ongoing battle.

We cannot surrender under our will power. It is not a matter of mustering up "all we got" and applying it toward the cause of surrender. That is not how it works. And even if it were, we do not have enough strength of will to make surrender work

Even if we could, by force of will, arrange our surrender to Jesus, then surrender would become a thing in which we could boast. And in its very existence, it would defeat its purpose.

Salvation is our first act of surrender. As we trust Jesus exclusively for the care of our eternal soul, we surrender to Him and receive the benefits of His love and care. Yet that surrender is not the end of the challenge.

Daily we are called upon to surrender. For as we declare Jesus our Savior and Lord, we step away from the throne of our lives and invite Him to rule us. Yet there are often parts of our life where we do not want to give up control and authority. So we enter the battle of submission.

Peter the disciple faced this dilemma. Too proud to have his feet washed by Jesus, he resisted.

> Peter said to Him, "You shall never wash my feet."
>
> Jesus answered him, "If I do not wash you, you have no share with me."
>
> Simon Peter said to Him, "Lord, not my feet only but also my hands and my head!"
> John 13:8-9

His resistance was temporary because he quickly realized that not surrendering placed him outside of Jesus' love. His unwillingness to submit was turned into a desire for even deeper submission.

This song takes us back to that time of salvation, where surrendering to Jesus meant releasing the burden of sin that was crushing us. At that moment, surrender was a great relief. Suddenly we could breathe as never before, and our hearts soared up out of sheer weightlessness.

As we live our lives, day in and day out, we do well to remember what that surrender felt like. We can apply that freedom and release to the other areas of our lives where we cling tightly to control. Undoubtedly we bear great burdens because of this insistence that we retain control of these aspects of our life.

Surrender is a frightening word. It speaks to lack of control, lack of choice, lack of protection. But let us remember to whom we are surrendering. Jesus, who loved us so much, He went to the cross and paid the penalty for our sins when He had done nothing to deserve such an injustice.

Let us sing the song again to renew our trust in our Savior and Lord. Our tight grip on the parts of our life that we refuse to release can only mean that we have an imperfect vision of the love of our Savior and that we have attributed to Him incorrect capabilities or motivations. He longs to take those parts of our lives and transform them into something much more fulfilling and far greater than we ever could.

As we surrender, we allow the Holy Spirit to work in our lives. We find that we grow to be more like Him who bled and died for us. And as a consequence, the surrender seems a much smaller burden, and love overwhelms our resistance. Let us dedicate ourselves to this path of surrender.

COUNT YOUR BLESSINGS

When upon life's billows
You are tempest tossed,
When you are discouraged
Thinking all is lost,
Count your many blessings
Name them one by one,
And it will surprise you
What the Lord hath done.

Johnson Oatman Jr.

W hat a reminder this great song brings to our hearts. It encourages us and admonishes us toward great thanksgiving. For, of all people, we are the most blessed.

It might be easy to let our thankfulness gravitate toward the material blessings we receive. Freedom, prosperity, and conveniences are all a source of blessings in our lives, blessings that we are often tempted to ignore or overlook and take for granted. But by far, the greatest blessings we have received are spiritual.

Our sins have been forgiven at no cost to us, but at great cost to Jesus. (2 Corinthians 5:21) The burden of sin we carried, which was crushing us underneath its massive weight, has been lifted off our backs and placed upon Jesus. At the cross, Jesus paid it all. We owe Him everything.

Jesus is preparing a place for us. When our life's journey is over, we shall step into that rest prepared for us by the very Son of God. He promised that He would go and get ready for us, and then we would be able to join Him. (John 14:6) We, who have never seen Him with our own eyes, will be face to face with Him and will see His glory for ourselves.

Jesus has defeated sin, death, and the world. (John 16:33) When we are upon life's billows amid the tempest, it is all too easy to think that they are all-powerful. Yet Jesus said that He has already overcome the world and the wicked power that drives it. So we can relax in the blessing that the hand that holds us is the victorious hand.

The Holy Spirit dwells within us. From the day of Pentecost onward, we have had a special guarantee that all the promises are true. Jesus sent the Holy Spirit as the deposit of good faith that all His promises would come true. (Ephesians 1:13-14) From this intimate location in our lives, the Holy Spirit gives us supernatural power to resist sin and to live a life that glorifies God.

We have access to the throne of God in prayer. We do not need any intermediary to represent the cares of our hearts to God. He hears our prayers - no matter how many of us may pray at one time. And when we don't know what or how to pray, the Holy Spirit steps in on our behalf and prays for us in ways that we can't even understand. (Romans 8:26)

These and many more blessings are all ours. Yet too often we forget that we have access to them and let them lie fallow, when we could be reaping a bountiful harvest of blessing.

We pray and God answers; sometimes No, but sometimes Yes. Then we are privileged to see the very hand of God at work in the world around us. It might be a sickness healed, or a loved one saved, or miraculous provision when none seemed available. We are children of the King and it pleases Him to do good for us.

But by far one of the greatest blessings is the knowledge that the One who holds us is sovereign, and nothing on this earth happens without His permission. He is leading history forward to the end He has intended, which will be the exaltation of His Son and the praise of every tongue ever created. There is no burden He did not foresee. There is no event He did not plan. All are part of His grand design that will bring final and ultimate glory to His name.

We would do well to count our many blessings. Name them, appreciate them. Remember that they all come directly from the hand of our loving God.

THERE IS POWER IN THE BLOOD

Would you be free from your burden of sin?
There's pow'r in the blood,
Pow'r in the blood;
Would you o'er evil a victory win?
There's wonderful pow'r in the blood.
There is pow'r, pow'r,
Wonder working pow'r,
In the blood of the Lamb.
There is pow'r, pow'r
Wonder working pow'r,
In the precious blood of the Lamb.

Lewis E. Jones

How often do the great hymns return to the blood of Jesus? And well they do, because only in the blood of Jesus do we find what we need most desperately: Power, forgiveness, acceptance, grace, and mercy.

The perfect blood of Jesus, innocent of any sin, spilled on our behalf is the gateway to the Kingdom of Heaven. There is no other way to be reconciled to God. A righteous God demands perfect justice, and in Jesus that requirement is satisfied.

The blood of Jesus paid our debt of sin. The hymn calls it our "burden" and indeed it did weigh us down like a pack of rocks. Slowly it was crushing us beneath the demands that we could not satisfy under our power. Absent a Savior, that burden led to an eternity without God.

But because Jesus lived His perfect life and exchanged His righteousness for our sinfulness, we now sing a different song. As children of the King, inheritors with Jesus, our outlook could not be more different than the path we were on.

> According to his great mercy, He has caused us to be born again to a living hope through the resurrection of Jesus Christ from the dead, to an inheritance that is imperishable, undefiled, and unfading, kept in heaven for you, who by God's power are being guarded through faith for a salvation ready to be revealed in the last time.
> 1 Peter 1:2-5

Because we have been cleansed by the blood of Jesus, sin's power over us is broken. No longer are we slaves to its oppressive power. We are free in Jesus and have a whole new range of options open to us. We can please the One who saved us. We can say "No" to the powers and principalities of this world and say "Yes" to Jesus.

We have the Holy Spirit living in us. He would not have come except that the blood of Jesus made a way for Him to abide in us. And He comes bringing spiritual gifts that give us purpose and meaning in the body of people who exalt the name of Jesus.

The blood of Jesus works wonders in our lives. It transforms the focus of our lives from selfishness and slavery to sin into an attitude of service and love for our Savior. Every day it gives us the power to live differently than we did before.

There can be no substitute. We cannot find a work-around. There is no alternate path to God. Remember the words of Jesus to doubting Thomas:

> Jesus said to him, "I am the way, and the truth, and the life. No one comes to the Father except through me.
> John 14:6

The way to God is through Jesus alone, and the wonderful power of His blood.

How often do we take it for granted? How often do we forget that we did not accomplish our new lives on our own? Has the memory of our former slavery to sin become so dim in our minds?

This great hymn brings to the front a truth that we need to be reminded of again and again. There is power in the blood of the Lamb.

HAVE THINE OWN WAY, LORD

Have Thine own way, Lord! Have Thine own Way!
Thou art the Potter, I am the clay.
Mold me and make me after Thy will
While I am waiting, Yielded and still.

Adelaide A. Pollard

Throughout the Bible, the image of the potter is used to describe God. Just as the potter exercises complete control over the clay, God exercises total sovereignty over our lives.

> But now, O LORD, you are our Father;
>   we are the clay, and you are our potter;
>   we are all the work of your hand.
> Isaiah 64:8

This great hymn reminds us of our right relationship with God. While He is our Father and we have entered into a peaceful relationship to Him, we are not His collaboration partners. He rules this world and all that happens upon it. Just as the clay does not advise the potter on how to effectively form the vessel, so too, we cannot make demands upon God.

Our proper position before God is submission. This song reminds us of what it means to be submissive to God. He knows what He is doing far better than we do. His plans for us are all good - even if we can't see it at the moment.

As we pray, we must remember what this song tells us. We know that God hears our prayers. Yet, His answers are not always immediate and sometimes He says "No" to our requests. In times like this, it is tempting to think that maybe He didn't understand completely, or that He's somehow punishing or testing us.

This is not God's way. He doesn't play with us for amusement or sport. When He answers our prayer differently than we want, it's because He has a plan that is better for us than what we are asking for. At this moment, our response should be "Have Thine own way, Lord."

Rather than focusing on what we want or what we have asked for, our submission allows God to mold us and shape us to look more and more like Jesus. When we resist this process, we do not learn the lessons we need to master, and inevitably have to go through the molding process again at another time.

Just as Jesus was submitted to the will of His Father, so we should emulate this and submit our lives as a blank canvas upon which God will create His masterpiece. The molding of God may come with discomfort and disappointment on our part, but when He reveals His handiwork, we will know we have been touched by the hand of a Master.

The last line of the song outlines the posture we should take. As we ask God to work in our lives, it is appropriate for us to yield to whatever He decides to do. We should not find ourselves in the place of giving conditional acceptance to God's power. We yield wholly to His plan and allow Him to work however He sees fit.

This may mean that our lives move in a different direction than we expected or dreamed. That's ok. God is interested in making His glory known, not meeting our expectations. Our job is to wait and be still. Truly this is a test of our confidence in God. When it seems that He is focused elsewhere, it's so tempting to try to fill in on His part and edge Him off the throne.

Yet the songwriter encourages us to wait and be still. God will answer in good time. And when He acts on our behalf, we know that He is doing what is best for us.

Have Thine own way, Lord. Have Thine own way.

THE OLD RUGGED CROSS

On a hill far away
Stood an old rugged cross;
The emblem of suffering and shame.
And I love that old cross
Where the dearest and best,
For a world of lost sinners was slain.
So I'll cherish that old rugged cross,
Till my trophies at last I lay down;
I will cling to the old rugged cross,
And exchange it some day for a crown.

George Bennard

The story of the cross never grows old. This song describes it well as rugged. Nothing about the cross merits much attention. But what happened on that tree changed the world more than any other event since God rested on the seventh day.

Looking at the cross we see the place of shame and punishment. It is a place toward which we were all rushing with all our might. Our sinful nature and rebellious actions made punishment the only possible outcome of our lives.

But Jesus interposed Himself, hanging on that cross in our place. And in doing so, He changed the course of our lives. No longer do we run toward the cross as our inevitable end, but now we come to the cross in love and remembrance.

Jesus hung on that cross when He had done nothing to deserve it. His life entitled Him to wear a crown of glory. Yet He chose to sacrifice Himself for people who were worthy of every bit of suffering and pain He endured.

The ugly, rugged cross became the ultimate showcase of love. On it, the most amazing exchange was made; our sin for His righteousness. Instead of enemies of God, we became children of God.

We look upon the cross with all its ugliness and symbolism of death and see our Savior hanging there. Suddenly the old rugged cross is transformed into a beautiful thing. It becomes the symbol of the love that we have received and the lengths to which God would go to redeem us.

"I will cling to the old rugged cross." Not because we are attached to it, but because it is the picture of who we were and what we have become in Christ. No other icon or symbol captures the love of God toward us in such a poignant manner.

We need to remember that we were deserving of that death, but He loved us anyway. We need to remember that our position before God was purchased through the suffering that occurred on the cross. We need to remember that the life we live now, we live through faith in the Son of God who gave Himself from us. (Galatians 2:20)

The old rugged cross keeps us humble. It keeps us thankful. It keeps us dependent upon the One who gives us the power to live a life that glorifies and honors Him.

So often the great hymns bring us back to the cross. This one does so more than most, and rightfully so. It is the essential truth of the Christian life. We who were enemies to God were redeemed and loved by the Savior who suffered in our place.

Remember the old rugged cross. Let it be the place to which we return again and again to remember and receive fresh love and strength.

> For God so loved the world, that He gave his only Son,
> that whoever believes in Him should not perish but
> have eternal life.
> John 3:16

Hold to the Savior who hung upon the cross. He is good and loving. He will never forsake us. He has gone to prepare a place for us so we can be with Him forever. And it all began upon the old rugged cross.

Turn Your Eyes Upon Jesus

O soul, are you weary and troubled?
No light in the darkness you see?
There's light for a look at the Savior
And life more abundant and free.
Turn your eyes upon Jesus,
Look full in His wonderful face,
And the things of earth
Will grow strangely dim
In the light of His glory and grace.

Helen H. Lemmel

J esus is the only antidote for a weary and troubled world. When all seems dark and hopeless, turning to Jesus brings light and life that restores our souls. So often we forget these truths and try to make our way by ourselves. Yes, the best answer is to turn our eyes back to Jesus.

In Jesus, we find love that knows no bounds. He alone has sacrificed Himself so that we might gain a right standing with God. He did what we could not do ourselves and offered it freely to us. We need only accept the gift and claim it as our own.

When the world around us is hard and challenging, we can always look upon Jesus. Our circumstances may not change, but our focus and our hope will. As the song says, there is always light to look upon Jesus. He is always available to us. It costs us nothing to look.

When we are lonely, we are reminded of His love. He has promised never to leave us and that He is preparing a place for us so that we can be with Him forever.

> Keep your life free from love of money, and be content with what you have, for He has said, "I will never leave you nor forsake you."
> Hebrews 13:5

When we are afraid, we hear Him say "no man can pluck you out of My hand." His grip is fast and secure and will never be broken. Regardless of what danger we face in this life, we know that our spiritual future will not experience any danger or risk but Jesus will overcome it and preserve us to the end.

> My sheep hear my voice, and I know them, and they follow me. I give them eternal life, and they will never perish, and no one will snatch them out of my hand. My Father, who has given them to me, is greater than all, and no one is able to snatch them out of the Father's hand.
> John 10:27-29

When we feel weak, He promises to send us the Holy Spirit, who comes upon us with power. We have been given the power to live new lives that are free of the tyranny of sin and equipped to love God. This power transforms us from who we were into who God is making us.

> "But you will receive power when the Holy Spirit has come upon you, and you will be my witnesses in Jerusalem and in all Judea and Samaria, and to the end

of the earth."
Acts 1:8

We turn our eyes to Jesus because He loves us. Nothing can shake that love and nothing can separate us from His love. When we spend our attention on Jesus, He changes our outlook on everything. We start to see ourselves through His eyes and our perspective is changed.

> For I am sure that neither death nor life, nor angels nor
> rulers, nor things present nor things to come, nor
> powers, nor height nor depth, nor anything else in all
> creation, will be able to separate us from the love of
> God in Christ Jesus our Lord.
> Romans 8:38-39

We are the people who have been changed because of Jesus. Our lives have taken a fresh trajectory, and we proceed under new power. Only Jesus offers the answers we crave. So we turn to Him, expectantly, in love and hope. His face is the most wonderful face we will ever see.

In the Garden

I come to the garden alone,
While the dew is still on the roses;
And the voice I hear falling on my ear,
The Son of God discloses.
And He walks with me,
And He talks with me,
And the tells me I am His own;
And the joy we share as we tarry there,
None other has ever known.

C. Austin Miles

S tep for a moment into the footsteps of Mary Magdalene. Her beloved Rabbi had been executed three days prior. Her world had turned from hope to despair in the matter of a weekend.

Early on Sunday morning, she came to the tomb where His body had been buried. To her shock and dismay, the stone had been thrown away, the tomb was open and the Roman soldiers who had been there the day before were nowhere to be seen. What had happened?

With her heart in her throat, she ran to the place where the disciples were hiding and grieving in their way. "The tomb is opened, come see!" Of all the disciples, only John and Peter believed her enough to take a look for themselves. They each went in and looked around, but there was nothing to see. So they left.

Mary, however, remained behind, alone with her sadness. The angels inside the tomb asked her why she wept and she answered "They have taken away my Lord." Seeing a man walking in the garden, she asked, urgently, if he knew what had happened. Where was the body?

The man answered with a single word. "Mary."

She recognized the voice. It was Him! He was alive! With a cry of anguish mixed with elation, she threw herself on Him, hugging Him, soaking His clothes with her tears.

Imagine how those next few moments would have felt for Mary. Her Jesus had come back from the dead. All the loss and despair she felt evaporated into hope. The desolation in her heart was overcome by love. He had not left her as she had feared but had done something wonderful.

This great hymn transports us through time to remember the events of John 20:11-18. We are invited to journey in our minds to the first moment of understanding the resurrection. Vicariously we experience the transformation of defeat into victory, hopelessness into victory.

As we try to connect with Mary's emotions, it is easy to stray into our own. We have received the same news that she did: He is not here. He has risen just as He said He would!

As we look for Him, we find Him. And in those moments we understand His love. We feel His power. We know that we are not alone and on our own. Our Anchor, our Rock is with us and will not leave us.

But mostly, we simply enjoy His presence. When we are with Him we feel safe and protected. We know that nothing can harm us while He is near. It is a feeling unlike any other in our lives. And it can only be experienced when we stand face to face with Jesus.

Mary's story reminds us over and over of the simple precious joy that comes when we discover Jesus is alive. In those moments, we gain a fresh sense of His love for us. That He was willing to die for us is one thing. But that He rose again and we can see and experience His presence is far better.

Cling to Jesus. Soak His garments with your tears of relief and joy and love. Hear Him tell you that you are His. Let your joy overflow at this moment and remind you again who you are.

WONDERFUL GRACE OF JESUS

Wonderful grace of Jesus,
Greater than all my sin.
How shall my tongue describe it?
Where shall its praise begin?
Taking away my burden,
Setting my spirit free
For the wonderful grace of Jesus reaches me.

Haldor Lillenas

A s with the blood of Jesus, great hymns often remind us of God's grace. It is a common theme for use to sing. For in Jesus is God's grace placed on display for all to see.

For a people born into rebellion against God, grace is a wonderful word. By our very nature we deserve punishment and judgment. But grace turns this equation around and gives us what we have not earned and do not deserve.

> For by grace you have been saved through faith. And this is not your own doing; it is the gift of God, not a result of works, so that no one may boast.
> Ephesians 2:8, 9

Grace puts all the benefits of heaven at our disposal. All of God's riches become available to us. From life eternal, to power to please God, to a new heart, we have it all because of Grace.

As Paul said in the letter to the Ephesians, grace is not a boasting matter. We have no grounds to lay claim or take credit for grace. It is God's gift to us. Our only action is to simply receive it.

Grace rests solely upon the work of Jesus. He is the one who purchased for us the benefits of God's grace. His perfect life and substitution sacrifice transferred all the benefits of God's grace to us.

Our sin was great, but His grace was greater. It covered our sin and made us presentable to God. Not only does it hide our sin, but it has paid the price for that sin and brings us clean and righteous before God.

How then shall we describe grace? It should be upon our tongue and part of our daily conversation. As the recipients of grace, we should declare it to whomever we speak. All the favor of God in our lives did not happen because of our own goodness. We should not ever attempt to take credit for it.

Grace points us back to the Grace-Giver. God has given us grace when we deserved judgment. He has given us gifts when we merited punishment. He has given us His Son when we had earned His judgment. No longer do we relate to God as our judge, but as our Father.

God's grace has completely turned around our life and given us a new future with Him in heaven. We look forward to this future of joy and praise. Our lives here on earth are but a prelude to that glory which is yet to come.

Yet we should be cautious lest we steal God's glory by claiming credit for His grace in our lives. If we allow this grace to become too familiar, we will begin to take it for granted. And if that seed takes root, we will begin to believe that the benefits of grace were ours all along.

This great hymn reminds us of the truth. We have been made alive through the grace of God.

> And you, who were dead in your trespasses and the uncircumcision of your flesh, God made alive together with Him, having forgiven us all our trespasses.
> Colossians 2:13

Without God's grace, this is how we find ourselves: Dead. We have no power to bring to God that assists His grace. We were unable to do anything for ourselves and are completely reliant upon Him for all that is good in our lives.

Decide today to remind yourself regularly of the grace of God. Dwell on what He has done for you and the gifts He has given you. Rehearse the great truth that through Jesus, God has redeemed us as the sign of His great love for us.

ACKNOWLEDGMENTS

My sincere thanks to Larry Horne who believed in this book even before I was fully committed to making it a reality.

Thanks to the Advanced team who added polish to the book: Eian Allardice, Diane Deacon, Eric Douglas, Debbie Hall, Linda Hobbs, Shirley McCullough and Tina Watts.

MORE GREAT BOOKS

If you found this little book helpful, check out more books I've written. Find encouragement for your faith and insight to inspire your worship. These books are available at your favourite online booksellers.

STUDY THE BIBLE - SIX EASY STEPS

In this book, I simplify Bible study into six straightforward and manageable steps you can easily master. Using clear explanations and detailed examples I'll show you how to uncover spiritual truth in the pages of your Bible.

Every step includes practice questions and guided answers that will build your confidence as your knowledge grows. Finally, you'll practice what you've learned with a guided study that illustrates the process and will answer your questions.

Thousands of people like you have used Study the Bible Six Easy Steps to dive into their Bible. If you like a step-by-step explanation, helpful examples, and guided exercises, then you'll appreciate this easy-to-follow approach to studying God's word.

Jesus Above All

In this short book, I'll breathe a fresh perspective into four familiar biblical encounters with Jesus and provide practical tools that will transform your daily worship. When you see Jesus clearly, your worship will never be the same again.

I wrote this book after an overwhelming worship experience in church. It started with a reading of the vision of Jesus in Revelation 4 and just spiraled from there. This book captures the awe and wonder and pure worship that I felt so that you can participate.

Faith & Miracles

Are you searching for a deeper faith? Do you want to live the life God intended for you? Discover the intimate relationship between your faith and God's miracles

Meet men and women in circumstances that cried out for a miracle. Whether God responded to their faith or acted to strengthen it, you'll discover how He cared about the condition of their heart. With insightful questions for each passage, journal your answers, or discuss them in a group to strengthen your faith and draw closer to God.

ABOUT THE AUTHOR

I write books for everyday Christians who want to build their faith. I believe that you can have a rich and rewarding spiritual life - even if you didn't go to seminary, or learn how to read Greek and Hebrew. The tools of the Christian faith don't have to be a mystery. That's where I want to help.

I cut through the confusing terms and present spiritual truth in everyday language. I'll show you how to get the most out of your Christian life with the tools and knowledge you already have. I'll break it down until it makes sense and you can do it for yourself.

I grew up in a pastor's home. Some nights, the dinner table felt like a seminary classroom. But the result was that I was given a deep love of God and the Bible from a very early age. As an adult, I built on that foundation by pursuing learning and study on my own. I still haven't gone to seminary, I don't think that's necessary to pursue God. I have impressed God's word on my heart and made it central in my life.

I've been studying the Bible myself for over 30 years. For more than 20 of those years I've been teaching others what I know. This experience, both of study and teaching, has shown me what everyday Christians want to know, and how they like to learn it. As an author, my purpose is to capture what I know and give it to you

I'd love to connect with you! You can join my fan list on my website at **https://www.dennis-stevenson.com/stay-in-touch** to learn about more books as they are published. This is the best way! You can also follow me online on my author page on Facebook at AuthorDennisStevenson.

Made in the USA
Las Vegas, NV
15 July 2023

74741150R00096